To Ann & Alan
A

D1391700

EIASFOO

Relish
SCOTLAND
SECOND HELPING

Original recipes from Scotland's finest chefs
and restaurants. Introduction by Tom Kitchin

First Published 2013
By Relish Publications
Shield Green Farm, Tritlington,
Northumberland, NE61 3DX.

ISBN: 978-0-9575370-0-2

Publisher: Duncan L Peters
General Manager: Teresa Peters
Design: Vicki Brown
Relish Photography: Kevin Gibson and Nicky Rogerson
Editorial Consultant: Paul Robertson
Senior Account Manager: Paul Bamber

Front cover photograph by Marc Millar

Printed By: Balto Print Ltd, Stratford,
London E15 2TF.

Relish
PUBLICATIONS

OUR HAND PICKED RESTAURANTS

As the proud owner of a Relish cook book, you may subscribe for your own personal Relish Rewards card which entitles you to a year's free membership.

You can access the Relish members' area on our website and find out what exclusive offers are available to you from the fantastic restaurants featured in our series of books throughout the UK. Look out for the Relish Rewards card icon at the end of each restaurant's introduction.

TO RECEIVE YOUR CARD
Simply register on our homepage www.relishpublications.co.uk or email relishrewards@relishpublications.co.uk and we will post your exclusive Relish Rewards card.

When you book just let the restaurant know that you are a member and take your card along with you.

WHAT ARE THE REWARDS?
The rewards will continue to be updated on the website so do check and keep in touch. These range from a free bottle of Champagne to free gifts when you dine. Relish will send you a quarterly newsletter with special discounts, rewards and free recipes. We are about quality not quantity!

All offers are subject to change. See the Relish website for details.

www.relishpublications.co.uk

004
CONTENTS

DESSERTS

RESTAURANTS

006
CONTENTS

DESSERTS

Coconut, Lime & Malibu Panna Cotta

Summer Strawberry Millefeuille

Triple Chocolate & Whisky Bavarois With
Butterscotch Sauce, Cranachan Ice Cream
& Candied Hazelnuts

Lemon Posset With Brandy Snap Fingers

Clotted Cream Panna Cotta With Grenadine
Rhubarb & A Tuile Twist

Chocolate Moelleux, Coconut Mousse
& Passion Fruit

Burnt Cumin Seed Custard With Poached Pears
& Sea Buckthorn Sorbet

Root Vegetables

Eton Mess

Crunchy Passion Fruit Cream, Coconut Sorbet,
Textures & Flavours Of Pistachio, Mango, Salt
& White Chocolate

Rhubarb Jelly, Poached Rhubarb, Milk Mousse,
Strawberry Sorbet

Pain Au Chocolat & Croissant Bread & Butter
Pudding With Vanilla Pod Ice Cream, Rhubarb
& Apple Compôte

Bunnahabhain Whisky & Honey Roast Parsnip
Crème Brûlée, Thyme Ice Cream

INTRODUCTION WITH TOM KITCHIN

I am very proud to be Scottish for many reasons. One is the fantastic larder and the beautiful produce available in this country but I am also incredibly proud of all the people who work tirelessly to provide myself and fellow chefs with the most outstanding produce from the Scottish land and sea. Our natural larder is like nowhere else I've ever seen and it is important that we all make the most of it by showcasing it to the world.

Scotland has really established itself on the international food scene over the past few years and I am very excited to be part of it. Before I opened my restaurant - The Kitchin in Edinburgh - with my wife Michaela, I was fortunate to work in some of the greatest restaurants in the world. I never failed to notice all the Scottish produce that we used. It is simply the best produce there is.

To make the most of each season, it is all about working with nature itself and allowing our unique produce and local cooking to speak for itself.

We have some truly fantastic fish and shellfish in Scotland as well as excellent game and wonderful meat along with berries and mushrooms to mention but a few. It is our responsibility as chefs of Scotland to respect the produce we work with and continue to provide our diners with some outstanding, imaginative cooking.

As our country is establishing itself as a gastronomic haven, this truly is an exciting time for Scotland.

Happy cooking!

Tom Kitchin

010
21212

3 Royal Terrace, Edinburgh, EH7 5AB

0845 22 21212
www.21212restaurant.co.uk

Paul Kitching's extraordinary Edinburgh restaurant with rooms - 21212 - has ridden a remarkable tidal wave of success since opening its doors in 2009 with its unique dining experience.

Only eight months after opening the doors, 21212 was awarded a Michelin Star for the wonderful food served by Paul and his team. The award was testament to the hard work, flair and imagination that goes into each dish served at the much talked about Edinburgh restaurant with rooms.

The Michelin Star followed hot on the heels of the honour of 21212 being named the 'Best New Restaurant in the UK' by Restaurant Magazine and the 'Most Stylish Hotel in Scotland' at the Style Awards. The AA and VisitScotland both grade 21212 as a five star restaurant with rooms and 21212 is the current 2012 CIS Scottish 'Restaurant of the Year'.

With four luxury bedrooms, a drawing room and two private dining rooms situated above the stunning 38-seater restaurant, it was quite an impressive feat to undertake such a sympathetic refurbishment.

The site, a beautiful Grade A listed Georgian townhouse, is split over four floors making it light, spacious and airy. Paul, his partner Katie and their business partners have invested £4.5m into the project and have been heavily involved in restoring the elegant townhouse to its former glory since inception, retaining many period features, while transforming the restaurant with rooms into a most comfortable and peaceful place to stay, with amazing food.

Relish Restaurant Rewards
See page 003 for details.

Scotland's current CIS Restaurant of the Year, 21212 is situated in a stunning Georgian townhouse only minutes walk from the heart of Edinburgh's shopping and theatre district.

The restaurant has held a Michelin Star since shortly after opening in 2009 and retained it annually since. The AA and VisitScotland both grade 21212 as a five star restaurant with rooms.

Scotish fish Platter

Cavier

Cue x4

fischo x4

SS

SCOTTISH FISH PLATTER
AN ASSIETTE OF ARMSTRONG OF STOCKBRIDGE BEST SMOKED FISH, FRESH CRAB MEAT FROM CAMPBELL & SONS IN PERTH, CAVIAR, LEMON & PISTACHIOS, WARM SLICED CUCUMBER

SERVES 4

 Springvale Watervale Riesling 2011, Grosset,
Clare Valley (Australia)

Ingredients

Fish

700g smoked salmon
100g smoked cod
100g smoked haddock
12 king prawns

50g caviar of your choice
100g white crab meat (picked)

Beurre Blanc

1 medium shallot (finely chopped)
3 thin slices of fresh ginger
50ml water
50ml sweet vinegar
50ml dry white wine
50ml Vermouth
100g ice cold butter (cubed)
lemon juice (squeeze of)

Horseradish And Caper Cream

2 tbsp creamed horseradish
2 tbsp whipped cream
4 tbsp mayonnaise
1 tsp vinegar
1 tsp capers
1 lemon (zest)
seasoning

Other Ingredients

spices of your choice
12 green pistachios
8 slices of cucumber
olive oil (to serve)
plain yoghurt (to serve)

Method

For The Fish

Slice the haddock, cod and salmon into fine slices and set aside.

Shell the prawns, cover in spices of your choice - we recommend using Tandoori, paprika and curry powder - and bake at 70°C for 15 minutes. Set aside.

You can get wonderful fresh crab meat at any food market or fish supplier and the caviar is a touch of luxury - go on treat yourself! Dot a little teaspoon size of crab and caviar with gay abandon, the more the better.

For The Beurre Blanc

Add liquids to a saucepan with shallots and ginger. Reduce on a high heat by three quarters.

Strain to a new pan and, on a low heat slowly whisk in the butter until fully *emulsified*.

Add lemon juice and season.

For The Horseradish And Caper Cream

Bind all ingredients together and chill.

To Serve

Place slices of smoked fish on a plate. Warm through the prawns, pistachios and cucumber in the *beurre blanc*. Drain, keeping the sauce, and pat dry. Assemble ingredients on fish plate, add caviar and crab. Return sauce to heat and foam, using a stick blender. Finish by drizzling *beurre blanc* foam over the plate. Serve the horseradish cream and yoghurt separately.

BEEF A LA GRECQUE

SERVES 4

🍷 *Terra delle Sirène Nero d'Avola 2006, Azienda Agricola Zenner, Sicily (Italy)*

Ingredients

4 x 200g Scottish fillet of beef
10ml of olive oil

Garnish

8 button mushrooms
8 spears white asparagus (peeled)
4 Anya new potatoes
100g leeks (finely sliced)
50g black pudding, 50g white pudding
garlic scented olive oil (for cooking)
seasoning

4 green olives, 4 black olives
50g feta cheese (grated)

Tomato Relish

1kg plum tomatoes (skinned and chopped to fine dice)
1 tbsp tomato paste
2 cloves garlic (diced), 1/2 onion (diced)
1 tbsp argon oil
1 tbsp white wine vinegar
10g cooked barley
25g porridge oats
dash olive oil

Oil Dressing

100ml extra virgin olive oil
1/2 garlic glove (crushed), 1/2 shallot (diced)
1/2 chilli (diced)
splash of sherry vinegar and lemon juice

Mushroom And Olive Parchment

150g button mushrooms
50g black pitted olives, 1/4 tsp caraway seeds
100ml natural yogurt
seasoning

Broad Bean And Potato Sauce

250g baby spinach
1 onion (diced), 4 cloves garlic (diced)
500g frozen broad beans
2 baking potatoes
150ml double cream
150ml vegetable stock

Method

For The Beef

Cook the beef fillet in the oven at 70°C for 55 minutes until medium rare. Set aside and rest until required.

For The Vegetable Garnish

Trim the mushrooms and cook on a low heat in garlic scented olive oil. *Blanch* asparagus and leek in salted water until tender. Refresh. Cook potatoes until soft, leave to cool and cut in half. Divide the white and black pudding into four even portions.

Set aside until you are about to serve.

For The Tomato Relish

Cook onion and garlic gently with a little olive oil until soft. Add the tomato purée, cook for 15 minutes and add chopped tomatoes.

Cover and cook for one and a half hours. Finish with barley, oats, argon oil and white wine vinegar to taste.

For The Olive Oil Dressing

Whisk together all ingredients, season with salt and pepper.

For The Mushroom Parchment

Blitz together all ingredients until smooth and spread everything on a *dehydrator* tray (available from all good kitchen equipment stores). Leave for four hours until dry and crisp. Alternatively, leave in oven at 40°C overnight.

Broad Bean And Potato Sauce

Cook onions, garlic and potatoes in salted water until cooked. Add defrosted broad beans and cook for a further 15 minutes. Add spinach and cook for one more minute.

Strain off excess water. Blitz in a blender until smooth and pass through a sieve. Add the cream and vegetable stock until it reaches a sauce-like consistency.

To Serve

Gently warm the beef fillets in olive oil, season and slice, *confit* white and black pudding in garlic oil. Reheat all vegetable garnish. Assemble as desired on plates.

Dress with the olive oil dressing, mushroom parchment and broad bean and potato sauce. Serve with the tomato relish separate, hot or cold.

Warm up olives in olive oil and sprinkle feta cheese on the dish just before serving.

CLASSICALLY GLAZED INDIVIDUAL LEMON TART, BLACK GRAPE JUICE

SERVES 4

 Muscat de Rivesaltes Mas Christine 2010
Languedoc-Rousillion (France)

Ingredients

Pastry

250g plain flour
50g butter
50g icing sugar
1 egg
1 tbsp water
4 x 10cm tart cases

Lemon Curd

750ml double cream
4 lemons
100g caster sugar
4 medium eggs

Raspberry Purée

200g red seedless grapes
100ml *stock syrup*

Grape Juice

2 x 250g punnets of raspberries
100ml *stock syrup*

To Garnish And Serve

plain yoghurt
icing sugar
hot frothy milk
nutmeg (grated)

Method

To Make The Pastry

Put flour, butter and icing sugar in bowl and rub together to create breadcrumbs. Add the egg and water and mix through until it comes together. Roll the pastry into a ball and rest for 30 minutes.

Once rested, divide into quarters and line four 10cm tart cases.

Bake blind at 180°C until cooked, set aside.

> **Chef's Tip**
> Clingfilm the tart case and fill with baking beans or rice.

For The Lemon Curd

Juice and zest lemons and place into a pan with the sugar. Add the cream in another pan, then put both pans on to heat.

Crack eggs into a bowl.

Once the lemon mixture and cream are hot, pass through a *chinois* over the eggs.

Whisk well and pour the mixture back into the cream pan.

Place back on heat. Whisk until eggs are cooked and the mixture has thickened. Set aside and cool.

For The Raspberry Purée

Place the raspberries and *stock syrup* in a pan. Cook down for 30 minutes. Blitz, pass, cool then put into a bottle.

For The Grape Juice

Blitz the *stock syrup* and grapes, pass through a sieve then set aside.

To Serve

Fill the tart case with the lemon mixture and level out with spatula. Heavily coat tart with icing sugar and caramelise with a blowtorch.

Dot alternate yogurt and raspberry purée around the outside of the plate.

Finish the tart with a dusting of icing sugar.

Serve grape juice on the side, topped with hot frothy milk and nutmeg.

020
THE AIRDS HOTEL & RESTAURANT

Port Appin, Appin, Argyll, PA38 4DF

01631 730 095
www.airds-hotel.com

The Airds has been privately owned and run for many years and is a member of Relais & Chateaux. Located on Loch Linnhe with the backdrop of the Morvern mountains, you could not want for a more stunning and peaceful hideaway, with a welcoming ambience from the moment you arrive. With 11 individually decorated bedrooms and suites, many of them with spectacular loch and mountain views and a two bedroom self catering cottage set within the grounds, there is a choice for everyone.

Enjoy full afternoon tea in one of the stylish lounges where a roaring fire in the winter will make you want to snuggle up with a good book or relax with an aperitif or indeed a night cap in the cosy bar, where there is an impressive display of Scottish whiskies just waiting to be tried. The garden stretches down to the loch where you can enjoy a simple stroll along the shoreline. For those feeling just a little more energetic, a game of croquet or putting is on hand before sampling the delights of our canapés prior to dinner.

The restaurant has three AA rosettes and a gold award with Eat Scotland, making it one of the finest in the country. It uses fresh, seasonal ingredients and local produce - only the finest quality will do. David Barnett heads an all Scottish kitchen brigade and says, "There is no better place to live and work than in the Highlands of Scotland with some of the best seafood in the world right on the doorstep and Scottish beef and highland game not matched anywhere else."

Relish Restaurant Rewards
See page 003 for details.

Breathtaking landscapes, incredible views down towards the loch, this remote and peaceful setting epitomises the West Coast of Scotland. Surrounded by one of the best natural larders in the world, the best local produce is sourced wherever possible and the restaurant has been featured consistently in the Good Food Guide for 37 years.

SEARED SCALLOPS WITH PANCETTA, BASIL & A LIGHT PARMESAN SAUCE

SERVES 4

 *Mourvedre Rose Collioure 2010
(France)*

Ingredients

Scallops

8 medium to large scallops
salt (to season)
rapeseed oil (to sear)
lemon juice (squeeze of)

Smoked Tomato Sauce

150g carrots (finely sliced)
40g celery (chopped)
1 clove of garlic (sliced)
20g butter
20g rapeseed oil
$^1/_2$ tbsp tomato purée
350g vine plum tomatoes (chopped)
100g smoked pancetta (whole)
1ltr smoked (or plain) chicken stock
(stock: 2kg chicken wings, cover with water, bring to a
boil, simmer for four hours and strain - skim off fat)
1 tbsp double cream

Parmesan Sauce

1shallot (finely sliced)
1 clove garlic (finely sliced)
25g butter
100ml white wine
400ml chicken stock
300ml double cream
80g grated parmesan

Yuzu Dressing

10ml yuzu juice (Sainsbury's speciality section)
40ml quality olive oil

Garnish

fresh basil
crispy pancetta
(cook wafer thin slices of pancetta between two trays
in the oven for six to ten minutes until crispy)

Method

For The Tomato Sauce

Sweat the carrots, celery, garlic, butter and oil and ensure not to colour. Add the tomato purée and cook for five minutes. Add the tomatoes and cook for a further five minutes. Then add the stock and the pancetta, reduce by three quarters, then remove the pancetta. Add the cream, blend until smooth and pass through a fine sieve.

For The Parmesan Sauce

Sweat the shallots, garlic and butter and again make sure it does not colour. Add the wine and reduce until there is no wine left. Add the chicken stock and reduce by half. Add the cream and bring to a boil, then pass through a sieve. Add the parmesan and simmer. Blend with a stick blender to create a foam.

For The Yuzu Dressing

Combine the yuzu juice with the oil.

To Serve

Season the scallops with salt and sear them in a very hot pan with rapeseed oil to achieve a golden colour. Turn each scallop and repeat on the other side, add a squeeze of lemon juice and baste them with the cooking juices.

Garnish the plates with the tomato sauce. Arrange the scallops on top with the crispy pancetta and garnish with basil. Finish with the parmesan foam and a little yuzu dressing.

> **Chef's Tip**
>
> I always get hand-dived scallops as fresh as possible, the better the quality of the scallops the better your dish will be.

ROASTED LOIN OF VENISON WITH TORTELLINI, BEETROOT, APPLE & A BRAMBLE JUS

SERVES 4

 McHenry Hohnen Three Amigos 2008 - Shiraz (Western Australia)

Ingredients

500g venison loin (trimmed)

4 x 90mm fresh pasta discs

1purple beetroot
1golden beetroot
1 beetroot

Tortellini Mousse

200g venison loin (diced)
100ml red wine
1 clove garlic (crushed)
1 cinnamon stick (broken)
2 egg whites
100ml port (reduced to a glaze)
170ml double cream
salt and ground white pepper

Savoy Cabbage

1 Savoy cabbage (root removed and finely sliced)
2 carrots (cut into thin strips)
4 banana shallots (finely sliced)
100g butter
100g chicken stock

Bramble Reduction

50ml water
15ml sweet wine
10g sugar
$^1/_2$ star anise
40g brambles
10g butter
100ml chicken *jus*

Pickled Apples

1 Granny Smith apple
125ml white wine vinegar
100g sugar

Method

For The Tortellini Mousse

Marinade the venison in the red wine, garlic, and cinnamon overnight. Discard the wine, keeping the cinnamon and garlic. Dry with a cloth. Blend the meat in a food processor for two minutes then add the egg whites and blend for one further minute. Add the reduced port and beat in the cream.

Leave in the fridge to set for one hour.

Spoon one dessertspoon of mousse on to the centre of each pasta disc and moisten the edges, folding over to create a half circle and pull the two corners together and pinch to stick. Cook for three minutes.

For The Cabbage

Boil the cabbage in water and put to one side on a draining tray. Sweat the shallots and carrots in the butter and add the chicken stock then reduce to a smooth, silky *emulsion*. Add the drained cabbage to this.

For The Bramble Reduction

Bring the sugar, water, wine and star anise to a boil. Add the brambles and bring back to a boil. Remove the anise, then add the butter, blend and then pass through a sieve. Mix one tablespoon of bramble *reduction* to four tablespoons of chicken *jus*.

For The Beetroots

Cut into 3cm discs and cook each type separately in seasoned water until tender.

For The Pickled Apples

Bring the white wine vinegar and sugar to a boil. Dice the apples and add to the vinegar and sugar. Remove from the heat and leave until required.

To Serve

Roast each portion of venison in a hot pan, in the oven and cook to your liking. Put the cabbage in a line on one side of the plate and arrange the beetroots on the other. Carve the venison into three equal pieces and garnish the plates with some pickled apples and some of the bramble *jus*.

POACHED NECTARINE WITH RASPBERRIES, HONEY SPONGE & A YOGHURT SORBET

SERVES 4

Ochoa Vino Dulce de Moscatel 2010
(Spain)

Ingredients

Nectarines

2 nectarines (not peeled)
400g sugar
1ltr water
40g glucose (from any good supermarket)

Raspberry Film

500g frozen raspberries
100g sugar
25g glucose
70g water
agar agar (available from any health food shop
or most Chinese supermarkets)

Yoghurt Sorbet

500ml natural Greek yoghurt
120g caster sugar
1 lemon (juice)

Garnish

fresh raspberries
honeycomb

Method

For The Poached Nectarines

Cut the nectarines in half and remove the stone. Bring the water, sugar and glucose to a boil then add the nectarines and cook for one minute or until the skin can be removed with ease. Leave to cool in the syrup.

Chef's Tip

Select perfectly ripe nectarines.

For The Raspberry Film

Place all the ingredients in a pan and boil for five minutes. Hang the purée in a muslin cloth and catch the clear red juice in a bowl. For every 100g of juice add 1g of agar agar and boil for three minutes. Pour on a flat tray to get a thin sheet of jelly. Cut into 15cm x 2cm strips.

For The Sorbet

Dissolve the sugar in 100g of yoghurt and lemon juice and whisk into the remaining yoghurt and churn in an ice cream machine.

To Serve

Cut the nectarines into three wedges per half and arrange in a zigzag down the plate and lay the film over them. Garnish with the raspberries, sorbet and some nuggets of honeycomb.

030
APPLECROSS INN

Shore Street, Applecross, Strathcarron, Wester Ross, IV54 8LR

01520 744 262
www.applecross.uk.com

t's no surprise the Applecross Inn was Scottish Seafood Pub of the Year 2012. Sustainable fish, such as creel-caught prawns (langoustines), are delivered direct from the fishing boats to the pub as are squat lobsters, crabs, oysters, scallops, lobster, hake, haddock and skate. And what better way to enjoy everyone's seaside favourite - fish and chips - than looking out over the sea to Skye.

There's plenty of choice and it's always busy, with food served all day, every day. Head chef Robert Macrae trained with Marco Pierre White and the Roux brothers before returning to his birthplace. As well as seafood, he and his chefs create classic dishes with local venison, wild mushrooms and some of the best meat in Scotland. Don't miss the steak and legendary onion rings!

For dessert, another seaside classic, homemade ice cream (golden syrup, bramble and apple, Kraken rum and raisin, whisky and honey...) or something traditional - cranachan, sticky toffee pudding, cheese and oatcakes.

The Applecross Inn is a lively, welcoming pub, crowned 'Best in Scotland' in the 2012 Good Pub Guide. There's a roaring fire in winter and outdoor tables in summer. Real ales include Bealach Na Ba, named after Applecross's stunning mountain road. Over fifty whiskies ensure a dram for every taste!

Judith Fish, proprietor for 24 years, offers year-round bed and breakfast with seven fresh ensuite rooms with sea views. Guests return year after year for the food, the welcome and the wild beauty of Applecross. And if you don't quite make it over to the West, try its sister, The Loch Ness Inn, Lewiston, near Drumnadrochit on Loch Ness.

Relish Restaurant Rewards
See page 003 for details.

"The ultimate wilderness inn in the Highlands."
Observer Magazine

SMOKED HADDOCK CHOWDER

SERVES 6 - 8

🍷 *Marques de Caceres Rioja Blanco Joven*
(Spain)

Ingredients

1 red onion
1 red, 1 yellow, 1 green pepper
3 sticks celery
1/4 celeriac
2 carrots
1 leek
65g butter
1 clove garlic (crushed with a pinch of salt)
1 sprig thyme
pinch each saffron and turmeric
400ml vegetable stock
salt
2 medium potatoes
3 fillets smoked haddock (diced)
750ml milk
200ml double cream
lemon juice (squeeze of)
pinch finely chopped herbs (chives, parsley, dill, tarragon)

Optional

hand-dived scallops (to arrange on top)
fresh warm bread (to serve)

Method

Applecross boasts some wonderful walks. There's no better end to a day of fresh air and views than a bowl of the Inn's famous haddock chowder!

Dice the onion, peppers, celery, celeriac, carrots and leek. Melt the butter in a large pan then add the diced vegetables, garlic, thyme, saffron and turmeric. Cover and cook over a low heat until everything is soft. Add 200ml vegetable stock and simmer for five minutes.

Meanwhile, peel and dice the potatoes. Cook separately in the remaining 200ml vegetable stock until just soft. Add a pinch of salt and turmeric.

Poach the haddock slowly in the milk, until almost boiling. Remove from the heat. Allow to cool for ten minutes.

Remove the haddock and strain the milk through a fine sieve. Add the drained potatoes, haddock and strained milk to the vegetables. Stir in the cream, lemon juice and herbs.

Check the seasoning. Serve steaming hot with bread.

As a treat, just before serving, panfry scallops in olive oil, drizzle with butter and lemon juice and arrange on top.

Chef's Tip

Finish the chowder with a measure of Ricard (Pastis).

APPLECROSS ESTATE VENISON LOIN ON APPLE & WHOLEGRAIN MUSTARD MASH WITH CREAMY SAVOY CABBAGE, PINE NUTS, PANCETTA LARDONS & A RICH RED WINE JUS

SERVES 6

Shiraz McHenry Hohnen, Margaret River (Australia)

Ingredients

Venison
6 x 200g venison loin (seasoned)
50g butter (per loin)

Jus
knob of butter
6 shallots (sliced)
6 mushrooms (sliced)
1 sprig thyme (leaves stripped)
1 clove garlic (chopped)
250ml red wine
50ml port
150ml beef stock
1 tsp redcurrant jelly

Savoy Cabbage
1 onion (finely sliced)
1 clove garlic (finely chopped)
1 sprig thyme
100ml vegetable stock
savoy cabbage (sliced approx 1cm thick)
20g pine nuts
50g pancetta lardons
knob of butter
1 tbsp double cream

Mash (per person)
1 portion hot mashed potato
1 dtsp apple purée
1 tsp wholegrain mustard

Method

Venison is the ultimate wild meat and there's no doubt it is free range. As you drive over the mountain pass to the Applecross Inn, look out for deer that stay well hidden on the hillside.

For The Venison

Preheat the oven to 200°C. Panfry the venison in a little oil until well sealed, then transfer to the oven for eight to ten minutes. Remove and allow to rest for ten minutes.

Return the venison to a hot frying pan and cook on all sides for two minutes. Reduce the heat, add 50g of butter per loin and continue to caramelise the meat for a further two minutes, taking care not to burn the butter. Keep any residue for the *jus*. Rest for a few minutes and carve.

For The Jus

Melt the butter in a frying pan. Cook the shallots, mushrooms, any caramelised venison trimmings, half the garlic and half the thyme over a medium heat until caramelised. Add the red wine and port and reduce over a fairly high heat to a syrup. Add the beef stock and simmer for about an hour. Add the rest of the thyme and garlic to the *jus*, along with the redcurrant jelly. Season and strain.

For The Savoy Cabbage

Sauté the onion and garlic with the thyme until soft. Add vegetable stock to cover. Add the cabbage and steam gently until slightly soft. Toast the pine nuts in a dry pan. Fry the lardons until crispy then finish with a little butter and add both to the cabbage. Season the cabbage. Stir in the cream.

To Serve

Combine the elements for the mash, and spoon a portion onto each plate. Place the carved meat on top and drizzle with the *jus*. Serve with the cabbage on one side.

> **Chef's Tip**
> Keep the local gamekeeper supplied with a good dram!

KRAKEN RUM & RAISIN ICE CREAM

SERVES 8

 Kraken Rum
(Caribbean)

Method

At the Applecross Inn, Kraken (a black spiced rum) is particularly popular, so ice cream chef Aron decided to use it to make his rum and raisin ice cream. This has fast become an Applecross Inn classic. Aron's recipe is adapted from the Malaga raisin ice cream served at London's Moro restaurant, where he trained.

Warm the Kraken and raisins in a small pan. Transfer to an airtight container and leave, preferably overnight, for the raisins to plump up.

Put the cream, milk, and cinnamon stick in a saucepan. Scrape in the vanilla seeds. Heat until just below boiling point. Remove from the heat.

In a mixer, beat the egg yolks and sugars until thick (approximately five minutes). Incorporate a quarter of the milk and cream mix into the sugar and eggs mixture, beating all the time.

Pour this mixture back into the milk and cream. Set over a gentle heat, stirring continually, until it reaches 80°C - any higher and you risk scrambling it.

Remove from the heat, pour into a bowl and place over iced water to cool rapidly.

Churn in an ice cream machine until firm, folding in the raisins and liquid towards the end.

Chef's Tip
Try reserving some of the raisiny rum to drizzle over the top of each scoop.

Ingredients

100ml Kraken rum
125g raisins
600ml double cream
300ml milk
1 cinnamon stick
1 vanilla pod (split lengthways)
7 egg yolks
100g soft, dark brown sugar
25g muscovado sugar
25g caster sugar

040
BALLATHIE
COUNTRY HOUSE HOTEL & ESTATE

Kinclaven, Stanley, Perthshire, PH1 4QN

01250 883 268
www.ballathiehousehotel.com

Ballathie Country House Hotel and Estate is situated on the banks of the River Tay in Perthshire. We have been a country house retreat for generations of guests and we have prided ourselves on our long history of looking after people, a tradition we now continue as a four star luxury hotel with a two AA rosette award-winning fine dining restaurant. Country sport lovers actively seek Ballathie out as their Perthshire base for golfing, fishing and outdoor breaks. We are experienced in organising fishing, shooting and golfing and can tailor-make a package to suit your own requirements. The quiet seclusion makes us popular with conference organisers and meeting planners. Our country setting is picture perfect for that extra special wedding venue. We were recently awarded Country Wedding Venue for the second year running.

Head chef, Scott Scorer, brings together the finest produce from Perth, around Perthshire and beyond to create a fresh twist on Scotland's classic cuisine. Home grown herbs, beef from the estate and fresh seafood, like hand-dived scallops, are delivered to our doorstep. We also boast a superb cheese selection. Find the perfect match for your meal with our extensive wine list, with a dozen wines available by the glass.

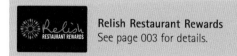

Relish Restaurant Rewards
See page 003 for details.

Ballathie Country House Hotel and Estate is situated on the banks of the River Tay in Perthshire. Head chef, Scott Scorer, brings together the finest produce from Perth, around Perthshire and beyond to create a fresh twist on Scotland's classic cuisine.

PRESSE OF CONFIT DUCK, SMOKED GRESSINGHAM DUCK BREAST, FOIE GRAS MOUSSE

SERVES 6

 Santa Florentina Pinot Gris Reserva Fairtrade Famatina Valley 2011 (Argentina)

Ingredients

Duck Confit

4 duck legs
2 cloves garlic
2 sprigs thyme
1 orange (zest)
1 bay leaf
1 ltr duck fat
soy sauce
2 tbsp veal *jus*
sea salt and black pepper
100g pistachio nuts (chopped)
50g breadcrumbs
2 beaten eggs
plain flour

Smoked Duck

2 duck breasts
salt and pepper

Foie Gras

1 lobe foie gras
142ml apple brandy
142ml double cream
salt and pepper

Fig Jelly

15 figs
500ml red wine
1/2 lemon (juice)
4 tbsp caster sugar
4g agar agar

Garnish

2 golden beetroot (cooked)
50g green beans
1 fig
3 peashoots
orange marmalade gel

Method

For The Duck Confit

Rub the duck legs with sea salt, black pepper, garlic, thyme, bay leaf and orange zest. Place the duck legs skin side down, cover and refrigerate overnight.

Preheat oven to 130°C. Remove marinade off the legs, cover with duck fat and cook for approximately three and a half hours until meat is tender. Remove from the oven and allow to cool. Once cool, strain off the fat and pick the meat off the bone. Place the flaked meat into a bowl, add a tablespoon of the duck fat, soy sauce and the veal *jus*. Season to taste. Set aside 150g of the duck *confit*, roll into spheres, *pané* in the pistachio breadcrumbs using the beaten egg and flour. Take the remainder of the mix and press in between two sheets of clingfilm to half a centimetre thick.

For The Smoked Duck

Score the fat of the duck breast and place skin down in a cold pan to start rendering the fat. Season with salt and pepper and cook until the skin is thin and crispy. Turn over and cook for a further three minutes, basting all the time. Take the duck and place it in a smoker and smoke for approximately three minutes. Remove, rest and cool.

For The Foie Gras Mousse

Slice the foie gras into 1cm thick slices, panfry the foie gras then *deglaze* the pan with apple brandy. Season to taste. Allow to cool slightly then, in a food processor, blend until smooth. Slowly add half of the cream. Remove from food processor and pass through a fine drum sieve. Semi-whip the remainder of the cream and fold in. Check for seasoning. Roll into cylinder shapes with clingfilm then refrigerate.

For The Fig Jelly

Combine the figs, red wine, lemon juice and caster sugar. Bring to a boil and simmer for half an hour. Blend until smooth then strain in muslin cloth. Take the clear *liquor*, add to the pan and add the agar agar. Simmer until dissolved and then pour onto a greaseproof tray. Place in the fridge to set.

Once the jelly has set, remove from the fridge and cut to the required shape. Unroll the cylinders of foie gras from the clingfilm and place on the edge of your pre-cut rectangle of jelly. Take the edge of the jelly and roll around the foie gras. Return to the fridge until ready to serve.

To Serve

Slice the duck *confit* into a rectangle. Assemble the rest of the ingredients on top of the *confit*.

ROAST TURBOT, CELERIAC FONDANT, CRISPY CHICKEN WINGS, HERB CRUSTED POTATOES

SERVES 4

Rully Blanc La Chatalienne Olivier Leflaive 2011
(France)

Ingredients

For The Turbot
1kg turbot
30g butter, 1tbsp oil
squeeze of lemon juice

Confit Chicken Wings
8 chicken wings, 1 pint duck fat
2 sprigs thyme

Celeriac Fondant
$^1/_2$ celeriac
860ml chicken stock (reserve 100ml for purée)
50g butter
thyme

Celeriac Purée
$^1/_2$ celeriac
1 onion
100ml double cream
100ml chicken stock
salt and pepper

Herb Crusted Potatoes
8 large waxy potatoes
290ml chicken stock
25g butter
283g brioche breadcrumbs
2 cloves garlic, 4 tbsp olive oil
150ml water
lemon (zest)
113g parsley, salt and pepper

Beetroot Purée
500g beetroot (cooked)
1 tbsp white wine vinegar, 50ml rapeseed oil

Garnish
200g spinach
beetroot crisps, red stem sorrel
beetroot purée
5 tbsp good quality veal *jus*

Method

For The Turbot
Trim turbot into four 250g portions. Set aside in the fridge.

For The Potatoes
Peel the potatoes and square them off into desired shape. Place potatoes in the cold chicken stock and butter and bring to a simmer. Cook until tender. Drain and set aside.

Place all dry ingredients in a food processor, blitz until combined. Add olive oil and slowly add the water until it forms a paste. Place between two sheets of greaseproof and roll until approximately 2mm thick. Refrigerate, then cut to the same size as the potato.

For The Celeriac Fondant
Remove outer skin of the celeriac, cut into 3cm slices (reserve half for the celeriac purée). Cut the celeriac into four medium size cylinders. Cook celeriac in the cold chicken stock and butter and bring to a simmer, cooking until tender. Drain and set aside.

For The Celeriac Purée
Finely dice the onion and sweat off with the garlic and thyme. Add diced celeriac and chicken stock and boil until the celeriac is soft to the touch. Place the celeriac in a food processor and blend until smooth, adding a touch of stock if required. Add the cream.

For The Confit Chicken Wings
Place chicken wings in a deep roasting pan, cover in duck fat and add the thyme. Place in a preheated oven at 130°C for approximately one and a half hours. Remove from the oven, set aside and allow to cool. Once cooled, remove the bones. Set on a tray and press for five hours.

For The Beetroot Purée
Place beetroot and white wine vinegar into a food processor and purée until smooth, slowly adding the oil. Place in a container and refrigerate until ready to garnish.

To Serve
Heat a non-stick frying pan, add a tablespoon of oil and place the turbot flesh side down and fry in the hot oil for three minutes or until golden brown. Turn over and add 30g butter. Cook for another minute, add a squeeze of lemon juice then season.

Place the *confit* chicken wings into a hot dry pan until the skin becomes crispy. Turn over and repeat the process.

Wilt the spinach and assemble all hot ingredients. To finish randomly spread the garnish over the plate.

PEANUT BUTTER PARFAIT

SERVES 6

 *Chateau Septy 2009, Monbazillac
(France)*

Ingredients

Peanut Butter Parfait

12 egg yolks
340g caster sugar
1 vanilla pod (seeds only)
1.4 litres double cream (semi whipped)
400g peanut butter
3 leaves gelatine

Chocolate Cookie

500g dark chocolate
100g butter
100g plain flour
5g baking powder
2.5g salt
4 eggs
350g light brown sugar

Chocolate Disc

680g white chocolate
680g dark chocolate

Toffee Sauce

400g caster sugar
small knob of butter
100ml double cream

Toffee Cream

toffee sauce
100ml double cream

Garnish

6 x 2cm x 8cm puff pastry rectangles
sugar spiral
popcorn
peanuts
caramelised bananas

Method

For The Peanut Butter Parfait
Whisk egg yolks and sugar, with the seeds from the vanilla pod, in a bowl over a *bain-marie* for three to four minutes until sugar dissolves and becomes pale and fluffy. Take off of heat and place in mixing machine. Whisk until cool. Add peanut butter to the *sabayon* and mix thoroughly.

In a machine, semi-whip double cream. Dissolve gelatine in cold water, then place in a pan with a little cream and melt. Add this to the peanut butter mix, then fold in cream and place in approximately 24cm x 4cm moulds.

For The Chocolate Cookie
Make a *sabayon* with eggs and sugar. Melt chocolate and butter in the microwave, stir at regular intervals. Sift flour, baking powder and salt and fold into *sabayon*. Add chocolate and butter to the mix - do not overmix. Place in piping bag and allow to rest for ten minutes. Pipe the size of a 10p and bake at 175°C for six minutes.

For The Chocolate Disc
Melt white and dark chocolate separately. Heat 75% of the chocolate in the microwave on half power. Stir every minute up to four minutes. Save remaining chocolate for *seeding*. Remove chocolate from microwave and stir to cool slightly.

Using a thermometer, check temperature of melted chocolate - it should be between 37°C and 43°C for white chocolate and 46°C and 48°C for dark chocolate. Add *seeding* chocolate in small handfuls continuously until desired temperature has been reached - 29°C to 30°C for white chocolate and 31°C for dark chocolate. This could take around 15 minutes. Make sure to stir the *tempered* chocolate and check the temperature.

Place dark chocolate in a piping bag. Position a silicone mat on a tray and randomly make squiggles all over. Place in fridge until dark chocolate is hard. Take white chocolate and spread evenly over the top, this should be thin and an even consistency and allow to set. Cut a large disc, then cut a smaller disc just off centre. Use a palette knife to lift off.

For The Toffee Sauce
Place sugar in a pan, heat until dissolved and it begins to caramelise. Add cream, butter and stir to combine on a low heat. Take off and allow to cool.

For The Toffee Cream
Semi-whip the cream, add toffee sauce and whisk to soft peaks.

To Serve
Cut parfait to desired length. Design the bottom of the plate with toffee sauce. Place chocolate cookie on the plate, parfait on top, place puff pastry on the plate opposite the cookie and pipe toffee cream onto it. Place caramelised bananas on top. Place chocolate disc in the parfait, place sugar spiral through and garnish with popcorn and peanuts.

050
THE BYZANTIUM

11 Hawkhill, Dundee, DD1 5DL

01382 221946
www.byzantiumrestaurant.com

S ituated in the Cultural Quarter of Dundee's vibrant west end, The Byzantium is leading a new wave of restaurants intent on establishing the City of Discovery as a culinary destination. After being a firm local favourite in the city for many years - 2009 saw a change of ownership and an extensive refurbishment of the restaurant in-keeping with the redevelopment of the city.

The restaurant offers a floor to ceiling, dual-aspect view out towards the West Port area of the city and its sleek design has been nominated for several architecture awards.

Under new ownership and the influence of chef patron Grant MacNicol, the restaurant has fused its Mediterranean roots with a more contemporary Scottish style of cooking. The Byzantium prides itself in using only the best 28-day mature beef, hand-dived seafood and a collection of exciting yet affordable wines.

The menus are extremely flexible and range from affordable two course lunches for £10 through to a full à la carte dining experience that embraces the freshest of local produce.

The philosophy is simple, to serve the best local produce in a casually sophisticated ambience.

Relish Restaurant Rewards
See page 003 for details.

Grant started his journey in the Highlands at Dornoch castle. After a series of 'stages' at a number of high profile restaurants, including Gordon Ramsay's York and Albany and The Kitchin, Grant was quick to establish himself as an exciting young talent. In 2007 Grant became 'Scottish Young Chef of the Year' and 'Highlands and Islands Young Ambassador'.

Appearances on Masterchef The Professionals and BBC2's The Adventure Show came thick and fast before Grant took the reigns at The Byzantium, Dundee.

HAND-DIVED KING SCALLOPS PLACED OVER CHICKEN & BLACK PUDDING BOUDIN WITH SAFFRON & WHITE ONION PUREE FINISHED WITH CONFIT CHERRY TOMATOES

SERVES 4

 Viognier, The Smoking Loon, 2011
(California)

Ingredients

12 hand-dived king scallops
butter

Purée

¹/₂ large white onion
0.5g saffron
100ml milk
200ml double cream
salt and pepper

Boudin

150g black pudding (diced)
700g chicken breast
500ml double cream
105g egg white
5g wholegrain mustard
seasoning

Confit Tomatoes

500m extra virgin olive oil
¹/₂ bulb fresh garlic
10g thyme
200g cherry tomatoes

Garnish

micro herbs

Method

For The Boudin

Blend the egg white, cream and chicken together until smooth. Add the wholegrain mustard and seasoning. Place in a large bowl and fold in the black pudding. Pour mixture into clingfilm and roll into a sausage shape with a diameter of around one and a half inches. Repeat wrapping process three times and tie off the ends. Wrap in foil and place into a deep tray. Add water until half of the boudin is submerged and place in oven at 180°C for 40 to 60 minutes.

For The Purée

Dice the onions and add the milk and cream in a heavy bottomed saucepan. Add the saffron and bring to a boil and simmer for 30 to 40 minutes. Strain the mixture out of the pan and blend until soft and smooth. The purée should be bright yellow. Season to taste.

For The Tomatoes

Place the oil, garlic and thyme in a pan on a low heat ensuring the oil never boils, and cook until tomatoes are soft but still holding their shape. This should take 40 to 60 minutes.

For The Scallops

Place pan on heat with a teaspoon of olive oil. Ensure the pan is very hot. Season the scallops and sear for 45 seconds on each side. Add a touch of butter and baste until golden in colour.

Chef's Tip

Opening a scallop can be tricky and it can be easy to tear the meat - most independent fishmongers would be more than happy to do this for you!

To Serve

Place the purée in bowl, slice boudin and place in centre. Ensure excess butter is disregarded from scallops and place on top of boudin. Garnish with cherry tomatoes and micro herbs.

PORK THREE WAYS: PORK BELLY, PORK CHEEK & CHORIZO & SWEET POTATO TORTE WITH TOFFEE APPLE, PICKLED TURNIP, BABY VEGETABLES & MUSTARD JUS

SERVES 6

 Gewurztraminer, Trimbach, Alsace 2007 (France)

Ingredients

Pork Belly

1kg skin-on pork belly
6 large pork cheek nuts (sinew removed)
1 carrot, 1 leek, 1 white onion (chopped)
1 stick celery
spices to taste (cinnamon, star anise, pink peppercorn etc)
15g rosemary
extra virgin olive oil
sea salt
1 garlic bulb

Torte

500g chorizo (sliced)
4 sweet potatoes
4 baking potatoes
250g butter
salt and pepper

Pickled Turnip

$^1/_2$ turnip
20g (2 sprigs) rosemary
150ml white wine vinegar
50g caster sugar

100g baby leeks
100g baby carrots

Toffee Apples

1 tin Chinese apples
red food colouring
100g granulated sugar
300ml cold water

Method

For The Pork Belly

Score the pork belly and rub with extra virgin olive oil, sea salt, rosemary and any other spices to taste. Chop the vegetables and place into a deep tray. Lay the pork cheeks on top of the vegetables and smother with the pork belly. Pour cold water into the tray until it just touches the underside of the belly and submerges the cheeks. You can also add cinnamon and star anise, if you wish, or stock. Place in a preheated oven and cook at 120°C for six to eight hours. The pork should be tender and pull away easily. To crackle the skin, up the heat to 200°C for the last ten minutes of cooking.

For The Torte

Peel the baking and sweet potatoes and slice wafer thin (about 3mm) using a mandolin. Line the bottom of a 25" square cake tin with parchment paper. Construct the torte with two layers of baking potato, one layer of sweet potato and a layer of sliced chorizo, pouring *clarified butter* between each layer. Season with salt and pepper. Repeat this process five or six times - applying pressure to each layer as you go. Ensure the last layer is baking potato - this will ensure even cooking and the top won't burn. Top with parchment paper and wrap in two layers of foil. Place the cake tin in a deep roasting tray and cook in the middle of the oven at 160°C for two hours. Once cooked, remove and allow to rest before taking out of the tin. Divide into six ample portions.

For The Pickled Turnip (Prepare the day before)

Add white wine vinegar, two sprigs of rosemary and caster sugar to a pan and boil for around eight minutes. Peel and *julienne* the turnip (slice very fine). Add the mixture and turnip to a pickling jar - this is best done 24 hours before serving.

> **Chef's Tip**
> It takes 36 hours to perfect our mustard *jus* - for homemade *jus* buy beef stock, add a spoonful of redcurrant jelly, a glass of good red wine, wholegrain mustard and reduce!

For The Toffee Apples

Ensure the baby apples are dry and make a caramel by boiling granulated sugar and 300ml water in a heavy bottomed pan for at least ten minutes. Just before the caramel turns brown, add a small amount of red food colouring and gently stir. Plunge bottom of the pan into cold water to stop the caramel from burning. Coat apples with caramel.

To Serve

Cook the baby leeks and carrots in simmering water for 45 seconds. Plate dish as pictured.

COFFEE & DOUGHNUTS WITH MARSHMALLOW FOAM & CHOCOLATE SPOON

SERVES 6

 Liqueur Muscat, Skillogallee (Australia)

Ingredients

Coffee Mousse

400ml double cream
3 whole eggs
3 additional egg yolks
250g dark chocolate
1 shot espresso or 1 tsp instant coffee
(dissolved in water)

Doughnuts

250g strong white flour
25g caster sugar
20g unsalted butter
1 egg
7g instant yeast
5g salt
75ml warm milk
65ml water
vegetable oil (for deep frying)

Marshmallow Foam

75g egg whites
150g caster sugar
45g water
1 sheet gelatine

Chocolate Spoon

50g dark chocolate
50g milk chocolate

Method

For The Mousse

Whip the cream and put to one side. Whisk the eggs and yolks together. Place the chocolate in a bowl and melt over a pan of simmering water until completely melted. Add coffee and stir. Allow to cool slightly and then fold into egg mixture. Allow to cool for a further ten to 15 minutes. After it has cooled, fold with whipped cream. Once finished, place into coffee cups three quarters full. The mixture should be light and airy. Place in fridge to set.

For The Marshmallow Foam

Soak the gelatine sheet in cold water. Boil the sugar and water. The mixture should reach 103°C on a thermometer. Whisk the egg whites until the peaks are soft. Add gelatine to the sugar and water mix until it completely dissolves. Slowly add the sugar and water liquid to the egg whites and mix until completely cool. Place in a piping bag and allow to cool in the fridge. Pipe over coffee mousse before serving.

Chef's Tip

When making marshmallow foam ensure the sugar is added as slowly as possible!

For The Doughnuts

Place all ingredients in a large mixing bowl. Holding back one quarter of the water, stir with your hands until dough is formed. Slowly add the remaining water and knead the dough in a bowl for four minutes. Tip dough out onto lightly floured surface and knead well for a further ten minutes until smooth and elastic. Place in a clean bowl, cover with a damp towel and allow to rise for an hour. Tip back onto floured surface and 'knock it back' by kneading a few more times. Roll dough out until 2cm thick and cut to the size you like your doughnuts. Place on a floured baking tray and allow to rise for an hour. Deep fry in sunflower oil at 180°C until golden brown and cooked in the middle. Dust with sugar whilst warm.

For The Chocolate Spoon

Melt chocolate in a bowl over a pan of simmering water. Pour chocolate into spoon moulds. Allow to cool.

To Serve

Serve as pictured.

060
CRAIG MILLAR @ 16 WEST END

16 West End, St Monans, Fife, KY10 2BX

01333 730 327
www.16westend.com

Born and educated in Dundee, Craig Millar started his career with Crest hotels in Buckinghamshire in the late eighties moving back north of the border three years later, working in several restaurants and hotels including Murrayshall House Hotel under the guidance of Bruce Sangster. In 1998 Craig joined up with Tim Butler for what was to be a 13 year partnership at The Seafood Restaurant in St Monans and they went on to open The Seafood Restaurant, St Andrews, in 2003. It was during this period that the pair won accolades such as SLTN Restaurant of the Year, AA Restaurant of the Year, AA Wine List of the Year, AA Seafood Restaurant of the Year, CIS Restaurant of the Year, Scottish restaurant awards 'Speciality Restaurant of the Year'. Both restaurants were also named 'Newcomer of the Year' in the Good Food Guide. Craig was also named 'Seafood Restaurant Chef of the Year" and he won "Taste of Scotland Lamb Challenge".

After a major renovation in June 2011 Craig and Tim went their separate ways with Craig taking sole ownership of the St Monans restaurant, renaming it Craig Millar @ 16 West End. Within the first eight months the restaurant picked up CIS Newcomer of the Year. The menu now includes more meat and game dishes rather than just specialising in seafood. Craig is also championing local produce, for example he sources fruit and vegetables from nearby Kellie Castle's Victorian walled kitchen garden.

Relish Restaurant Rewards
See page 003 for details.

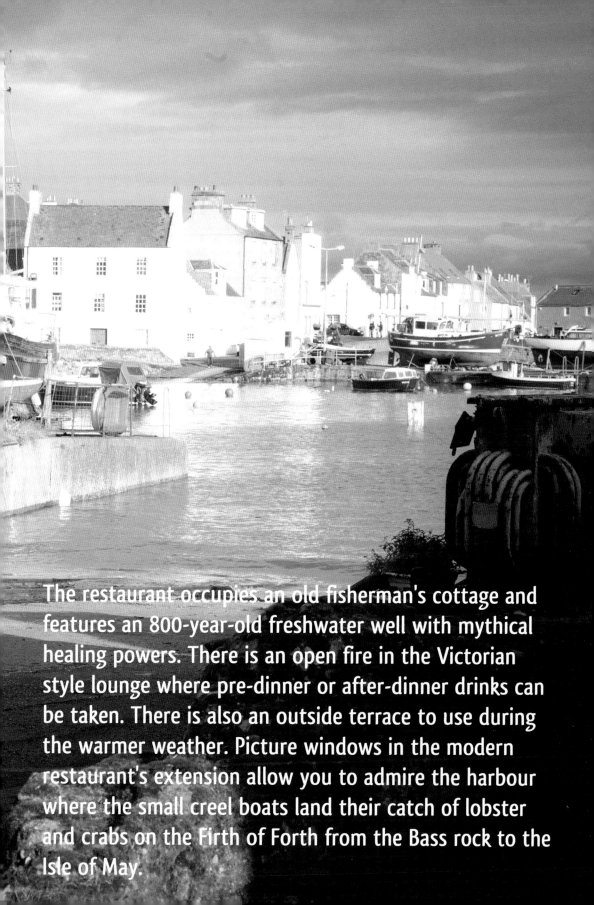

The restaurant occupies an old fisherman's cottage and features an 800-year-old freshwater well with mythical healing powers. There is an open fire in the Victorian style lounge where pre-dinner or after-dinner drinks can be taken. There is also an outside terrace to use during the warmer weather. Picture windows in the modern restaurant's extension allow you to admire the harbour where the small creel boats land their catch of lobster and crabs on the Firth of Forth from the Bass rock to the Isle of May.

BEETROOT CURED TROUT, PURPLE POTATO, QUAIL'S EGG, DILL MAYONNAISE

SERVES 8

🍷 *Bourgogne Rosé, Cuvee Margonton, Olivier Leflaive, 2008 (France)*

Ingredients

Trout
1 side of sea reared trout (skinned and pin boned)

For The Cure
500g beetroot (peeled and roughly chopped)
1tsp fennel seeds
250g caster sugar
500g sea salt

Mayonnaise
2 egg yolks
1tsp Dijon mustard
1tbsp white wine vinegar
200ml rapeseed oil
1tsp dill (chopped)
salt

16 quail eggs

Beetroot
1kg beetroot
50ml white wine vinegar
apple juice

Garnish
salad cress
500g purple potatoes

Method

To Cure The Trout (Prepare the day before)

Place all ingredients for the cure into a food processor and blend to a smooth paste. In a tray, coat the trout with the cure, clingfilm and place in the fridge for ten to 12 hours. Turn the trout over, re-cover and place back in the fridge for another ten to 12 hours. Wash off the cure, pat dry and set aside.

For The Mayonnaise

In a food processor, add the egg yolks, mustard, vinegar and salt. Blend and slowly add the oil until thick. Finally, add the chopped dill and check seasoning.

For The Quail's Egg

Bring a pot of water to a rolling boil, add the eggs and cook for two and a half minutes. Remove and place in a bowl of iced water. De-shell and set aside.

For The Beetroot

Wash the beetroot and place in a pan with the vinegar and some salt. Cover with cold water, bring to a boil and simmer for 20 to 30 minutes until the beetroot is soft (this will depend on the size of the beetroot). Cool then peel the beetroot and cut into 1cm dice. Add the trimmings to a food processor and blend with a little apple juice to form a smooth purée. Set aside.

To Cook The Potatoes

Clean the potatoes and boil in salted water until cooked. Refresh in iced water, peel and dice into 1cm cubes.

To Serve

Slice the trout to give five slices per portion and arrange randomly on a large plate. Spoon five small dots of mayonnaise and beetroot purée and place the warm potato and cold beetroot cubes on top. Halve the quail eggs, season with a little sea salt and arrange four halves per plate. Garnish with salad cress and serve.

> **Chef's Tip**
> The addition of fresh breakfast radish would go well with this dish, adding another texture.

HAND-DIVED SCALLOPS, CAULIFLOWER PANNA COTTA, CURRIED RAISIN PUREE, CEP, CRISPY CAULIFLOWER, PEA CREAM

SERVES 4

 Muddy Water, James Hardwick, Riesling, Waipara Valley 2008 (New Zealand)

Ingredients

12 large hand-dived scallops (*shucked*)

Panna Cotta

2 heads cauliflower
1 ltr milk
1 ltr double cream
8g agar agar (250ml water)
salt

Curried Raisin Purée

250ml rapeseed oil
1 Granny Smith apple (thinly sliced)
$^1/_4$ onion (thinly sliced)
$^1/_2$ stalk of lemongrass (thinly sliced)
1 kafir lime leaf
1 tbsp madras curry powder
250g golden raisins (soaked in boiling water for two hours)

Deep Fried Curried Cauliflower

150g plain flour
10g fresh yeast
330ml cold water
1 tsp madras curry powder
1 head cauliflower
plain flour (to dust)
1 tbsp curry oil (from curried raisin purée recipe)

Pea Cream

250g frozen peas
150ml water
salt

Garnish

4 cep mushrooms (sliced)
knob of butter
salad cress
400g mash potatoes

Method

For The Panna Cotta

Thinly slice the cauliflower and place in a pan with the milk and cream over a medium heat. Simmer until the cauliflower is soft and the liquid has reduced by half. Transfer the cooked cauliflower and reduced cream mixture to a blender and purée until smooth. Season with salt. Remove two tablespoons of the purée and set aside. Add the agar agar to a pan with 250ml of cold water. Bring to a boil whilst constantly whisking. Add the mix to the puree then transfer to a 15cm by 25cm by 4cm roasting tray lined with clingfilm. Place in fridge to set, then dice into 2cm cubes.

For The Pea Cream

Place the frozen peas into a blender with the water and a pinch of salt. Blend until smooth then pass through a fine sieve. Set aside.

For The Curried Raisin Purée

Place half the oil, onion, apple and lemongrass into a pan over a medium heat. When it starts to boil, remove from the heat. Add the remaining oil, lime leaf and curry powder and allow to infuse for 30 minutes. Strain through muslin. Soak the raisins in boiling water for two hours, drain and discard the water, transfer raisins to a blender and purée with a little of the curry oil (retain some curry oil for the deep fried curried cauliflower).

For The Deep Fried Curried Cauliflower

Mix the water, yeast and curry powder together and slowly whisk in the flour. Leave in a warm place for 20 to 30 minutes. Floret the cauliflower into pieces no bigger than a 20 pence coin and *blanch* in salted boiling water. Refresh in iced water. Drain then reserve. Now add the curry oil. Allow to infuse for 20 to 30 minutes. Dust in flour and coat with the batter. Deep fry at 180°C until golden brown, place onto kitchen paper and season with salt.

To Serve

Heat mashed potatoes and place in a piping bag. Heat a large non-stick frying pan with a little rapeseed oil. Season scallops and sear on both sides for 45 seconds to one minute depending on size. Remove from pan, add the cep mushrooms with a little knob of butter and season. Dress plate as shown in picture.

Chef's Tip

To heat up cold mash potato, simply heat a pan with a little cream until it boils then add the mash and some butter and mix with a rubber spatula until hot and smooth.

CHOCOLATE CREMEUX, SALTED CARAMEL, SESAME TUILE, ROASTED BANANA SORBET

SERVES 8

Bowmore Darkest, 15 year old, Islay Malt Whisky (Scotland)

Ingredients

Crémeux

190ml milk
190ml whipping cream
60g caster sugar
4 egg yolks
1 sheet gelatine
175g dark chocolate drops
100g dark chocolate (for coating)
8 x 7cm diameter rubber moulds

Sorbet

8 ripe bananas (with skins on)
190g caster sugar
$^1/_2$ tsp salt
$^3/_4$ tsp lemon juice
375ml water

Salted Caramel

250g caster sugar
125ml double cream
200g unsalted butter
$^1/_2$ tbsp sea salt

Sesame Tuile

100g caster sugar
50g sesame seeds
50g butter
30g plain flour
40g orange juice
1 orange (zest)

Method

For The Sorbet

Preheat oven to 180°C. Place unpeeled bananas in a roasting tray lined with greaseproof paper. Roast for about 30 minutes. Peel then add the banana into a blender with sugar, salt, lemon juice and 375ml water. Purée and pass through a fine sieve. Freeze in an ice cream machine.

For The Crémeux

In a pan, bring the milk and cream to a low simmer. In a mixing bowl, whisk the egg yolks and sugar together and pour the hot cream and milk mix into the egg yolk mix. Return this to the pan and heat to 82°C, stirring continually with a wooden spoon. Soften the gelatine in iced water. When pliable, squeeze out the excess water and add to the egg mixture. Pour the hot mixture over the chocolate and whisk until it has emulsified. Fill eight, 7cm diameter dome rubber moulds with the chocolate mix and freeze for about two hours. Melt the remaining chocolate over a *bain-marie*. Un-mould the crémeux and coat in the melted chocolate. Place in fridge until required.

For The Salted Caramel

Melt the sugar in a heavy bottomed pan and bring to a dark amber colour. Whisk in the butter then add the cream and salt. Set aside and allow to cool.

For The Sesame Tuile

Melt the butter and combine with all other ingredients and chill. Spread onto a non-stick, heat proof rubber mat and bake at 180°C until golden brown. Allow to cool and break into pieces.

To Serve

Place a spoonful of salted caramel on each plate and spread across the plate with an offset spatula or a spoon. Place the crémeux slightly off centre. Use a piece of the tuile as a base for a quenelle of sorbet and place another on top. Enjoy!

Chef's Tip

A variety of ice creams will work with this dessert. We recommend you use peanut butter and banana as we do in our restaurant.

CRINGLETIE HOUSE

Edinburgh Road, Peebles, EH45 8PL

01721 725 750
www.cringletie.com

On approaching Cringletie House up the winding, single track road, an air of serenity, tranquillity and peace descends upon the guests.
There is almost an urge to get out of the car and walk the final 100 metres, if only for the slope of the drive! As soon as the building comes into sight guests are invariably struck by its beauty. This pretty, pale pink sandstone building, with the large original, astragalled sash windows, exhumes the character of the typical Scottish Baronial mansion with its romantic turrets.

The house was designed and built by famous Scottish architect David Bryce in 1861 as a shooting lodge for the Wolfe Murray family, replacing an older house that was erected in 1661. Fortunately, the characteristic wall plaques were preserved and adorn the current house together with a number of new plaques which are so typical for Bryce's buildings.

The walled garden is something very special. It dates back to 1661 when the first Cringletie House was built. At the time it provided fruits, vegetables and flowers for the inhabitants of the house. Nowadays, we still grow our own vegetables and herbs, soft and hard fruits, potatoes and flowers but on a slightly smaller scale. Flower beds have been planted with scented lavender and roses. There is a games area to occupy young and old with pétanque, chess and draughts.

Patrick Bardoulet joined Cringletie House in September 2011 where he took on the full responsibility of the kitchen and obtained three AA rosettes by the AA Restaurant Guide within 12 months. Head chef Patrick began his culinary career at the age of 15, working at Le Chateau Montvillargenne in the north of Paris, a former residence of Baroness Jeanne de Rothschild. In 2007 he moved to Scotland where he appreciates the wonderful, flavoursome produce we have to offer and which inspires his classical cooking along with modern techniques.

Relish Restaurant Rewards
See page 003 for details.

Patrick Bardoulet joined Cringletie House in September 2011 where he took on the full responsibility of the kitchen and obtained three AA rosettes by the AA Restaurant Guide within 12 months.

TRILOGY OF SCALLOPS
TARTARE, SOUFFLE & SEARED

SERVES 4

🍷 *Pinot Gris Clos Jebsal VT 2007 Domaine Zind Humbrecht, Alsace (France)*

Ingredients

Soufflé

4 scallops
double cream (equal in weight to the scallops)
pinch salt and pepper
1 egg white

Tartare

4 scallops
1 shallot
1 orange (zest)
1 grapefruit (zest)
1 lemon (zest)
1 tsp olive oil
20g butter
pinch salt and pepper

Seared Scallops

4 scallops
1 tsp olive oil

Foam

scallop stock (reduced)
trimmings from the scallops
1 carrot (chopped)
1 shallot (chopped)
25ml whipping cream

Method

For The Soufflé

Blend together the scallops with the cream, a pinch of salt and a pinch of pepper. After blending until smooth, add the egg white. Spoon the mixture into four small greased ramekins. Keep in fridge until required.

For The Tartare

Dice the scallop *brunoise* style with the shallot. Dice the citrus zest and add to the scallops with the olive oil and a pinch of salt and pepper. Spoon into buttered clingfilm and roll into a sphere. Store in fridge. Prepare half an hour in advance to allow to solidify in the fridge.

For The Foam

Keep all trimmings from scallops. Add one chopped carrot and one shallot. Cover with water and bring to a boil for ten minutes. Reduce down to syrup consistency, then add 25ml of whipping cream. Season to taste with salt and pepper and foam with hand blender.

For The Seared Scallops

With one minute to go for the soufflé, sear the scallops on a high heat for 30 seconds on each side.

To Serve

Put the soufflé in the oven at 95°C for six minutes. Serve as pictured.

PIGEON HARMONY WITH A PRESS OF PEAR, POTATO, ARTICHOKE SERVED WITH LEEK, MORELS & CASSIS JUS

SERVES 4

Saint Emillion Grand Cru 2009 Chateau Barrail
du Blanc. Bordeaux (France)

Ingredients

2 woodland pigeons

Stock

bones from the 2 pigeons
1 carrot (chopped)
$1/2$ leek (chopped)
1 onion (sliced)
1 bay leaf
sprig thyme
1 clove garlic
bottle red wine
2 tbsp crème de cassis

For The Legs

300g *crepinette*
1 tbsp olive oil

Terrine

2 large pears
stock syrup (200g sugar and 300g water)
4 globe artichokes
500ml vegetable stock
400g large potatoes

Morels

12 fresh morels
1 shallot (chopped)
3 tbsp double cream
$1/2$ leek (finely chopped)
knob of butter

Garnish

sage or bay leaf
sprig rosemary
sprig thyme
filo pastry cone filled with chopped and
panfried baby leeks (optional)

Method

To Prepare The Pigeons

Remove the breast, fillet and legs from the pigeon. Set aside in the fridge. Retain the bones for the stock.

For The Stock

Roast the pigeon bones for ten minutes at 200°C in the oven. Mix together the chopped carrot, half the leek and the sliced onion in a separate bowl with the thyme, garlic and bay leaf.

Place the herbs and vegetables together in the bottom of a heavy saucepan. Add the roasted pigeon bones. Cover with a bottle of red wine. Simmer for 45 minutes. Pass through a fine sieve. Reduce the liquid to the consistency of syrup. Add two tablespoons of crème de cassis.

For The Legs

Sauté the legs until lightly browned. Cover with olive oil and cook at a very low temperature for two and a half hours. Remove the meat from the bones. Dice the fillet and add to the cooked leg meat. Wrap in a *crépinette* and place on a tray ready to be baked.

For The Terrine (Prepare the day before)

Peel the pears and cook in the stock syrup for ten minutes, but keep them firm. Cut and trim the artichokes and cook in vegetable stock for 45 minutes. Peel, slice and deep fry the potato. Then, in a small terrine, make a layer of deep fried potato, a layer of artichoke, then a layer of potato, a layer of pear and finally another layer of potato. This needs to be done a day before use.

For The Morels

Check the morel mushrooms and clean them under running water. Then, sauté with a teaspoon of chopped shallot and add a little bit of cream. In another pan, add a knob of butter and the finely chopped leek and sauté until tender.

To Serve

Place the legs in the oven for seven minutes at 180°C. Cook the breast on both sides with olive oil and butter for about one and a half minutes on each side. Re-heat the terrine. Arrange as pictured.

CHOCOLATE INDULGENCE WITH COCOA SHORTBREAD & TONKA BEAN CREME BRULEE

SERVES 6

🍷 *Champagne de Castelnau Brut NV Epernay (France)*

Ingredients

For The Chocolate

45ml milk
45ml double cream
15g egg yolk
15g caster sugar
50g dark chocolate (chopped)

Crème Brûlée

40ml double cream
2 tsp ground tonka beans
7g caster sugar
15g egg yolk
1/2 leaf gelatine (leaf of 2.5g)

Shortbread

20g soft butter
16g light brown sugar
16g plain flour
4g cocoa powder
20g ground almonds
pinch salt

Method

For The Chocolate

Bring the milk and cream to a boil. Mix the yolk and sugar, then pour the hot milk and cream into the yolk and sugar mix and cook until 82°C. Pour onto the chocolate. When the mix is still slightly warm, pour into stainless steel cylinders or ramekins 5.5cm diameter and 5cm high.

For The Crème Brûlée

Bring the cream to a boil with the tonka beans and leave to infuse for about an hour. Pass through a fine sieve and bring back to a boil. Meanwhile, mix the egg yolk and sugar and cook until it reaches 82°C. Then, add the half gelatine leaf and pour the mix into a piping bag.

For The Cocoa Shortbread

Mix all of the ingredients together in a mixing bowl. Place greaseproof lining paper on a baking tray and pour on the mix and bake for 15 minutes at 180°C.

To Serve

Arrange as pictured.

080
CUCINA

Hotel Missoni, 1 George IV Bridge, Edinburgh, EH1 1AD

0131 220 6666
www.hotelmissoni.com

Hotel Missoni Edinburgh opened in June 2009 in the centre of the city, at the corner of George IV Bridge and the Royal Mile, just steps from Edinburgh Castle. Ideally located in the beautiful old town, it offers spectacular views over the city and is in an ideal position for many of it's attractions, 'designed by fashion legend Rosita Missoni to give a true taste of the Missoni lifestyle'. Hotel Missoni is uncomplicated, iconic and contemporary, offering those luxury touches that really matter. Established as Scotland's most stylish five star hotel, Hotel Missoni has built its reputation on warm, friendly, hospitality tailored to the individual.

Mattia Camorani has been head chef of Cucina at Hotel Missoni Edinburgh since it opened. Mattia, originally from Imola in Bologna, brings his Italian upbringing and passion to each and every dish created at Cucina. Working closely with his mentor, internationally renowned Giorgio Locatelli, Mattia has created a collection of menus that bring the quality and values of the Italian family kitchen to a five star restaurant experience. Mattia Camorani's innovative Cucina menus present a contemporary vision of Italian dining based on beloved and authentic ingredients. His strong emphasis on sharing and tasting very much reflects the Italian way of life.

Here, life is beautiful.

Relish Restaurant Rewards
See page 003 for details.

The heart of Hotel Missoni is the award-winning Cucina; a vibrant, bustling Missoni designed restaurant. The service is friendly, relaxed, welcoming and attentive. Using the freshest seasonal ingredients and hearty flavours, Mattia Camorani creates authentic modern cooking inspired by classic Italian cuisine, with a range of seasonal and regional menus on offer. With consistently high standards, the food and wine on offer brings a genuine taste of Italy to the heart of Edinburgh.

PHEASANT RAVIOLI WITH PHEASANT & ROSEMARY JUS

SERVES 4

 Uvaggio Coste della Sesia Rosso, Proprietà Sperino (Doc) Piemonte 2008 (Italy)

From Coste della Sesia, a lesser known wine zone in Piemonte, this blend of Nebbiolo, Vespolina and Coratina will present the perfect balance of structure and depth of flavour with a certain supple, vibrantly refreshing body. The dominant notes of cherries and plums give way to Nebbiolo's darker, deeper character of winter spices and cooked mushrooms, with a long and elegant finish.

Ingredients

Filling

4 pheasant breasts (cut in half and season on skin side)
40g pancetta (finely chopped)
1 banana shallot (finely chopped)
175ml dry white wine
2 tbsp parmesan cheese
1 egg
4 tbsp double cream
1 tbsp vegetable oil
salt
black pepper

Pasta

500g strong flour (sieved)
3 large eggs, plus 2 extra (large) egg yolks (all at room temperature)
pinch salt

Jus

350g pheasant bones
60g shallots
60g carrots
10g garlic
sprig rosemary
20g butter
20g tomato purée
20g plain flour
1 ltr pheasant stock or chicken stock

Garnish

fresh rosemary (chopped)

Method

For The Filling

Preheat to oven to 180°C.

Heat an ovenproof, non-stick pan until it smokes. Add a tablespoon of vegetable oil and the pheasant (skin side down). Cook it quickly until the skin turns golden. Add the pancetta and shallot. Turn the pheasant over and continue to cook for few more minutes. Add the white wine and cook until the alcohol has evaporated. Transfer the pan to the preheated oven for three to four minutes, until the pheasant is cooked through, but be careful not to over-cook. Let the breasts cool down a bit then place in a food processor and blend to a rough paste.

Place the mix in a bowl with two tablespoons of parmesan cheese and one whole egg. Season if necessary. Add four tablespoons of double cream, mix and put it in the fridge until cold. With your hand, roll the mix into little balls. You should have enough for 32.

For The Pasta

Sieve the flour into a clean bowl and then, onto a clean surface, tip into a mound with a well to form the 'fontana di farina' (fountain of flour). Add the eggs, egg yolks and a pinch of salt. Break the yolks and, using your hands, gradually bring the flour into the mix until it is combined into a ball. Knead the dough until it becomes springy.

Wrap the dough in clingfilm and leave in the fridge for 12 hours. Once the filling is ready, you should roll the pasta out. If you have a pasta roller, this is easiest, but you can use a rolling pin. Roll it out and fold it on itself. Repeat this several times, getting gradually thinner each time. Finally roll it to around half a centimetre thick and cut into circles, roughly 8cm in diameter. Brush half of these with a beaten egg.

For The Jus

Cut the pheasant bone into small cubes and let them reach room temperature. Heat them in a large shallow pot. Roast the bones with vegetable oil making sure they cover the bottom of the pot evenly. Add the carrots, shallots and butter and let them cook. Add the rosemary, garlic then add the tomato purée and continue to cook, while gently mixing and adding the flour. Finally, add the stock and reduce for 45 minutes. Strain the *jus* to the correct consistency.

To Serve

Assemble the ravioli by placing the rolled up filling on the centre of a pre-cut circle of pasta. Top with a second sheet of pasta and press down lightly around the edges of the filling. Cook in salted water. Meanwhile, heat some of the sauce in a saucepan. Drain the ravioli and place in the saucepan with the sauce and toss around. Serve immediately with some fresh chopped rosemary.

MONKFISH ALL'ACQUA PAZZA

SERVES 4

🍷 *Langhe Arneis, Cristina Ascheri, Piemont 2010
(Italy)*

*Dry, pleasant palate of great freshness, delicate
wine with remarkable balance and finesse.*

Ingredients

150g - 200g monkfish (per person)
1 head Cos salad
300g fresh tomatoes (diced)
80g green olives (diced)
100ml white wine
400ml fish stock
vegetable oil (for cooking)
40g extra virgin olive oil
1 lemon
30g parsley (chopped)
salt
black pepper

Method

For The Monkfish

Preheat the oven to 180°C.

Cut the Cos salad so it fits in the plate that you are using to
serve the fish.

Heat one or two ovenproof non-stick pans to a medium heat.

Add the vegetable oil to the pans and season the fish with salt
and black pepper.

Cook the fish in the pan for about two minutes on each side,
depending on the thickness of the fillet.

Turn the fish over and place in the oven for about three minutes
on each side.

Take the pan out of the oven, pour the wine in the pan and let
it evaporate. Add the fish stock and green olives.

Let the sauce reduce for a few minutes then add the diced
tomatoes.

Take the fish out of the pan and let it rest on a chopping board.

In the meantime, cook the Cos salad in boiling water for few
seconds, drain well and place in a pan with olive oil and season
with salt and lemon juice.

Chef's Tip

Try to source Sicilian olives to add to the authenticity of this
summer dish.

To Serve

Place the Cos salad at the centre of a dish and place the fish
on top.

Finish the sauce by reducing it a little bit more if needed.
Season with salt black pepper and extra virgin olive oil. Add the
lemon juice to taste.

Spoon the sauce over the fish.

ZABAGLIONE WITH WHITE TRUFFLE

SERVES 6

Recioto di Soave Le Colombare, Pieropan (Docg)
Veneto 50cl 2008 (Italy)

An unusual re-interpretation of the Soave grape,
Garganega is a dessert wine with a distinctive
personality. Opulent and voluptuous, yet
maintaining aromatic floral characteristics so
typical of the Garganega grape. This makes it an
ideal companion to white truffle, intense, heady,
yet at the same time delicate and elegant.

Ingredients

8 egg yolks (from 8 eggs that have been stored
in an airtight container with white truffle)
160ml marsala wine
80g white sugar
white truffle (for garnish)

Method

For The Zabaglione

Place the yolks, sugar and marsala wine in a deep, round
bottomed, stainless steel bowl.

Place the bowl over a pan of boiling water and whisk the
mixture continuously for eight to ten minutes, being careful not
to overheat. The mixture will become very light and creamy as
you whisk more air into it and will expand in size. Whisk until
there is a light 'custardy' texture.

Chef's Tip

When placing the bowl over the pan of boiling water,
ensure that the bottom of the bowl does not touch the
water as this will overheat the mixture.

To Serve

Pour the contents of the bowl into a Martini glass and serve warm.

Shave white truffle on to the top to complement and
strengthen the flavours.

090
THE DINING ROOM

28 Queen Street, Edinburgh, EH2 1JX

0131 220 2044
www.thediningroomedinburgh.co.uk www.smws.co.uk

The Dining Room opened in 2004 as part of The Scotch Malt Whisky Society's beautifully restored Georgian townhouse at 28 Queen Street. The Society had been looking to unleash the creative spirit and natural talent of executive chef James Freeman who had impressed members for many years at their Leith venue, The Vaults. James continued to build on his reputation and helped develop The Dining Room as one of the main fine dining destinations in the capital.

Although the restaurant is open to non-members, feedback from regular members gave us the confidence to build our 'crafted' style - emphasising natural, honest cooking with simple elegance. Broadly speaking our cooking style is modern European, built upon a firm respect for sound technique and understanding the science behind our methods. Crucially, we use good marriages of flavour, allowing ingredients to really shine together. Complementary combinations and contrasting texture is where the magic is.

A collective approach is encouraged, valuing contributions and critique from customers, waiters and chefs alike. This collaboration, along with good sourcing, regular dish changes as seasons turn and allowing spontaneity, all help keep the menu alive.

The Dining Room is featured in the Michelin guide and is reviewed as having 'modern accomplished cooking'. They were also shortlisted for Restaurant of the Year 2012 by SLTN and 'Imbibe' shortlisted them for Wine List of the Year 2011. The main thing is they like to keep it fun and lighthearted. "It's just cooking - and we intend to enjoy it."

Relish Restaurant Rewards
See page 003 for details.

A new addition to the two existing menus is The Taster Menu. Five courses are not only matched with wines, but there is also an option to have five single cask whiskies matched to the dishes. These are selected from the Scotch Malt Whisky Society's world's largest selection of single cask whiskies. The Society, which won Independent Whisky Bottler of the Year in 2012, offers a range of more than 150 different single cask whiskies to its members but in The Dining Room they become available to the wider public.

HAND-DIVED SCALLOPS, SQUID, HAM & CELERY BOUILLON

SERVES 4

Chardonnay, Morning Fog, Wente Vineyards, 2010 (California)
Whisky: 9.67 - Granny's Kitchen Dram, 10yo Speyside SMWS Single Cask

Ingredients

6 scallops
4 baby squid (cleaned and scored)

500ml vegetable nage (vegetable stock)

1 onion, 1 carrot, 1 celery (finely chopped)
virgin rapeseed oil
700ml of water
sprig tarragon
sprig thyme
1/2 tsp coriander
2 strips lemon zest
glass white wine

Ham And Celery Bouillon

1 ham hock (soaked for 12 hours)
400ml vegetable nage
2 heads celery
1 onion, 1 carrot
1 bay leaf, 1 sprig tarragon, 1 tsp fennel seeds
virgin rapeseed oil

For The Radishes

6 icicle radishes
100ml vegetable nage
virgin rapeseed oil

Method

For The Nage (Make the day before)

Simmer the *mirepoix* (finely chopped vegetables) in 700ml of water for 25 minutes with the tarragon, thyme, coriander, lemon zest and a glass white wine. Leave overnight, then strain.

For The Ham And Celery Bouillon

Braise the ham hock in 400ml of the vegetable nage with onion, carrots, a head of celery, bay leaf, fennel seeds and tarragon for approximately four hours. Strain and retain stock. Whilst still warm, remove ham from bone and discard any fat or sinew.

Chop half the remaining celery roughly and sweat briefly. Add the ham stock and cook gently for 45 minutes until it has reduced by half. Strain through muslin.

Peel and de-seed the remaining celery, retaining the leaves, cut into neat cubes. Poach in the remaining 100ml of nage until tender, glaze with rapeseed oil and keep warm.

For The Radishes

Wash the radishes and poach in the remaining 100ml nage until tender, glaze with rapeseed oil and keep warm.

For The Fish

Cut the scallops in half and fry at high temperature for 45 seconds on each side.

Fry the squid for 30 seconds in hot oil.

To Serve

Reheat the ham hock with celery leaves and a little ham bouillon. Arrange the celery, radishes, ham and celery leaves in the bottom of a bowl. Place the scallops and squid on top. Pour over a little ham and celery bouillon, drizzle with a little rapeseed oil. Serve extra bouillon on the side.

LOIN OF RED DEER VENISON WITH LAPSANG SOUCHONG, OLOROSO SHERRY SAUCE, BABY BEETROOT & POTATOES DAUPHINE

SERVES 4

Jean-Claude Boisset - Beaune 1er Cru Les Greves 2007 (France)
Whisky: 66.37 - Building Site Worker's Dram, 10yo Highland SMWS Single Cask

Ingredients

Venison

440g venison loin
1 tsp lapsang souchong tea
1 orange (zest of)
1 tsp thyme leaf
1 tsp coarsely ground pepper

Sherry Sauce

200ml venison stock
200ml Oloroso sherry
mirepoix (250g, equal quantities of onion, carrot and celery)
1 star anise
1 sprig thyme
10 peppercorns
1 strip orange zest

Vegetable Garnish

8 baby beetroots
1 head chicory
1 dtsp sugar
4 shallots

Potato Dauphine

22g butter
44g plain flour
88g water
275g very dry mashed potatoes
1 egg
1 egg yolk
salt and white pepper

Method

Dry the lapsang souchong tea, orange zest, thyme leaves and ground black pepper for one hour, then grind in a spice grinder.

For The Sauce

Caramelise the *mirepoix* gently, then *deglaze* with the sherry, reduce by half. Add the venison stock and reduce by three quarters. Whilst the sauce is still hot, infuse with one star anise, one small sprig of thyme, ten peppercorns and one strip of orange zest. Leave for five minutes then strain through muslin.

For The Potatoes Dauphine

Bring butter and water to a boil, add flour then quickly beat in the egg and the egg yolk. Fold in the mash and seasoning. Chill for one hour.

For The Vegetables

Roast the baby beetroots in a foil bag for 45 minutes, peel and keep warm.

Roast the shallots in their skin for 20 minutes, peel then caramelise. Keep warm.

Blanch the chicory for five minutes in boiling, salted water. Cut into four pieces and caramelise heavily with white sugar. Keep warm.

To Serve

Make quenelles out of the the dauphine mix, then fry in clean oil for five to seven minutes until golden brown.

Arrange vegetable garnish on warm plates, carve the venison, seasoning the cut side with Maldon salt. Put a little sauce on each plate. Arrange the venison and potato dauphine.

PISTACHIO CAKE, LEMON CURD, PRESERVED RASPBERRIES, WHIPPED MASCARPONE

SERVES 4

🍷 *Dulce Monastrell DO Yecla Bodegas Castano 2008 (Spain)*
Whisky: 7.77 – French Patisserie In A Bluebell Wood, 20yo Speyside SMWS Single Cask

Ingredients

Lemon Curd

4 lemons (zest and juice)
270g caster sugar
200g butter (cubed)
4 eggs
1 egg yolk

Whipped Mascarpone

100g mascarpone
150g double cream
1 vanilla pod
40g caster sugar

Preserved Raspberries

150ml raspberry vinegar
1/2 vanilla pod
1 strip lemon zest
150g caster sugar
24 raspberries

Pistachio Cake

100g semolina
200g ground pistachio nuts
1 dtsp pistachio compound
50g plain flour
1 tsp baking powder
125ml light olive oil
100g unsalted butter (melted and cooled)
3 eggs
1 lemon (zest and juice)

Method

For The Lemon Curd

Whisk together lemon juice, zest, sugar and eggs. Heat to simmering point then stir in the butter little by little.

For The Whipped Mascarpone

Whisk all ingredients together until light and fluffy.

For The Preserved Raspberries

Briefly boil the raspberry vinegar, sugar, vanilla and lemon zest. Allow to cool and pour over the 24 raspberries.

For The Pistachio Cake

Mix the semolina, pistachio nuts, flour and baking powder together.

Add the olive oil to the melted butter. Whisk the eggs and sugar until pale and then slowly whisk in the pistachio compound and the oil and butter.

Stir in the dry ingredients and the lemon zest and juice.

Bake in a greased and lined tray at 160°C for 45 minutes.

Leave to cool and cut as desired.

To Serve

Arrange all elements on a plate as in the picture.

100
HAMILTON'S BAR & KITCHEN

16-18 Hamilton Place, Stockbridge, Edinburgh, EH3 5AU

0131 226 4199
www.hamiltonsedinburgh.co.uk

When Colin Church and Martin Luney opened Hamilton's in 2008, they set upon Stockbridge as their ideal location. Taking its name from the old Scots word for wooden footbridge - after the original bridge that crossed over the water of Leith into the small village - work on the Stockbridge that we see today began in 1801. With a village atmosphere and only ten minutes from the city centre, Stockbridge is definitely one of Edinburgh's hidden gems. The area has an obvious bohemian vibe and many artists, poets and writers, including Sir Henry Raeburn, poet James Hogg and more recently, singer Shirley Manson have made it their home. The affluent area is as renowned today, for its stylish boutiques, independent galleries and many eateries, as it was 200 years ago.

As an independent bar and kitchen, Hamilton's couldn't be better suited to the area. With the famous Stockbridge clock adorned on their customised Roy Lichtenstein inspired mural, Hamilton's represents all that is great about Stockbridge; with individual style, a relaxed atmosphere and great food and drinks.

Hamilton's prides itself on a menu that changes with the seasons and takes advantage of local suppliers while always remaining innovative with a home cooked feel.

Head chef Sean Canning, born to an RAF father, travelled extensively as a child and as a result has an eclectic array of culinary influences - but it was the time spent in the Highlands which caused him to fall in love with Scottish produce, a passion he retains to this day.

Relish Restaurant Rewards
See page 003 for details.

With the famous Stockbridge clock adorned on their customised Roy Lichtenstein inspired mural, Hamilton's represents all that is great about Stockbridge; with individual style, a relaxed atmosphere and great food and drinks.

SEARED SCALLOPS WITH CARROT & LEMONGRASS PUREE & CHORIZO FOAM

SERVES 4

Sauvignon Blanc (South Africa)
Medium bodied, so as to not overpower the scallops,
with nice acidity to cut through the chorizo

Ingredients

Carrot And Lemongrass Purée

4 large carrots (diced)
$^1/_4$ tsp sea salt
$^1/_4$ tsp white pepper
2 large shallots (fine diced)
50g unsalted butter
25ml whipping cream
1 lemongrass stalk (split)

Chorizo Foam

100ml fresh fish stock
100ml whipping cream
150g dolce chorizo (diced)
25g unsalted butter
1 garlic clove (fine diced)
1 large shallot (fine diced)
1 tsp heather honey
1 sprig lemon thyme

Seared Scallops

12 hand-dived scallops (roe removed and dried
on kitchen paper)
$^1/_4$ tsp sea salt
1 tbsp vegetable oil
50g unsalted butter

Method

For The Carrot And Lemongrass Purée

Heat the butter in a small saucepan until it starts to bubble, then add the shallots, lemongrass and carrot. Cook on a low heat for approximately three minutes, then add cream and continue cooking on a low heat until the carrots are soft. Remove the lemongrass stalk and then blitz the mixture in a food processor until smooth. Season with salt and pepper.

For The Chorizo Foam

Heat the butter in a small saucepan until it begins to bubble. Add shallots, garlic and cook until soft. Add the chorizo and honey and continue to cook on a low heat until the honey starts to caramelise. Add fish stock and thyme and reduce by one third. Add whipping cream, bring to a simmer and remove from heat. Leave this to infuse for half an hour then pass through fine muslin, check seasoning and leave in a warm place.

For The Seared Scallops

Heat a non-stick sauté pan over a high heat, add oil and half the butter. When the pan starts to smoke, add scallops flat side down - **do not move them** until you start to see a light, caramel coloured crust forming around the underside. When this happens they are ready to turn. Once turned, remove from the heat and add the remaining butter. Lightly baste the scallops for around a minute and serve immediately.

Chef's Tip

Once the scallops hit the pan - do not move them. You will interrupt the caramelisation of the crust.

To Serve

Assemble as in picture.

ASSIETTE OF PORK - ROAST PORK BELLY, CRISPY PIG'S CHEEK, CHARGRILLED PORK LOIN & STORNOWAY BLACK PUDDING FRITTERS WITH THYME ROASTED PEARS & GARLIC MASH

SERVES 4

 New World Red

Ingredients

Roast Pork Belly
400g - 600g pork belly (boned, skin on, finely scored)
2 cloves garlic, 1 sprig thyme
1 tbsp groundnut oil
1 clove, $^1/_4$ tbsp black peppercorns
$^1/_4$ tbsp coriander seeds, $^1/_2$ tbsp rock salt

Crispy Pigs' Cheeks
4 small pigs' cheeks
500ml (approx) chicken stock
bouquet garni
panko breadcrumbs
3 free range eggs (lightly beaten)
plain flour (for coating the cheeks)
salt and pepper
vegetable oil (for deep frying)

Black Pudding Fritters
250g Stornoway black pudding (rolled into 12 balls)
150g plain flour
100ml good dark ale
50ml sparkling mineral water (ice cold)
white wine vinegar (dash of)
salt and pepper

Thyme Roasted Pears
3 pears (unpeeled, cored and quartered)
4 sprigs fresh thyme (roughly chopped)
2 tbsp olive oil, 2 tbsp honey
salt and pepper

Garlic Mash
300g King Edward potatoes
$^1/_2$ bulb garlic
50ml whipping cream
50g unsalted butter
salt and pepper

Method

For Roast Pork Belly (Prepare the day before)
With a pestle and mortar, grind up all herbs and spices with the groundnut oil and rub all over the pork. Leave to marinade in the fridge for at least four hours (overnight if possible). Place on a baking tray and roast in a preheated oven 220°C for 20 minutes then reduce heat to 190°C and roast for a further 35 to 45 minutes until the skin is crispy.

Chef's Tip
Make multiple scores on the skin and massage with salt. Leave for at least four hours prior to roasting to ensure a good crackling

To Braise And Fry The Pigs' Cheeks
Place in an ovenproof dish and cover with the chicken stock, add the bouquet garni and season well. Wrap tightly in foil and allow to cook in a low oven (approximately 140°C) for four hours or until very tender and then allow to cool in the liquid. Once cool, pat dry and remove any excess fat. Dip the cheeks in to the flour, then beaten egg, then breadcrumbs and deep fry at 180°C until crisp.

For The Black Pudding Fritters
Pour the ale, water and vinegar into a bowl and sift in flour. Whisk and season well. Lightly roll the pudding in a little plain flour and dip into the batter mix. Deep fry at 180°C until golden and crisp. Season well and dry on kitchen paper before serving.

For The Thyme Roasted Pears
Mix all the ingredients well in a bowl. Pour onto a non-stick baking sheet, arrange evenly and roast in a hot oven (approximately 240°C) for 40 minutes or until tender.

For The Garlic Mash
Before boiling the potatoes, peel the garlic. Add these to the water and boil with the potatoes until tender. After draining, mash together. The garlic will be fairly mild and slightly sweet. Finish with the cream and butter and season well.

To Serve
Assemble the dish and serve with pear crisp and pork *jus* if desired.

CHOCOLATE & ALMOND TRUFFLE TORTE WITH POPCORN ICE CREAM & TOASTED HAZELNUT PRALINE

SERVES 8

🍸 *Bourbon Old Fashioned*
Caramel and muscovado flavours to complement the chocolate with bitters to cut through the sweetness of the praline

Ingredients

Chocolate Torte

60g ground almonds
150g unsalted butter
6 free range eggs
75g caster sugar
25ml Amaretto
350g good quality dark chocolate

Popcorn Ice Cream

250ml full fat milk
125ml double cream
2 free range egg yolks
100g caster sugar
75g salted popcorn
25g unsalted butter
sea salt

Hazelnut Praline

75g caster sugar
1 tbsp water
50g chopped hazelnuts
lemon juice (squeeze of)

Chef's Tip

Adding a few drops of fresh lemon juice into the caramel will guarantee a brittle praline

Method

For The Chocolate Torte

Lightly toast almonds in a hot oven or grill. Butter a 23cm spring form tin and lightly dust with a tablespoon of ground almonds and shake off any excess. Beat the eggs and sugar until light and creamy until the volume of mixture is doubled. Melt the butter in a small saucepan with the Amaretto. Over a *bain-marie*, melt the chocolate, butter and Amaretto mix until the chocolate has completely melted and allow to cool to room temperature.

Fold half the egg mixture into the chocolate then pour this mix back into the remaining egg mixture. Add the toasted almonds and fold gently - **do not over mix**.

Pour the batter into the baking tin.

Sit the tin in a deep baking tray and place in a preheated oven (180°C). Carefully pour in enough hot water to come up about one third the height of the tin and bake for 25 to 30 minutes. Carefully lift the cake out of the waterbath and allow to cool in the tin on a wire rack.

For The Popcorn Ice Cream

Pour the milk and cream into a large saucepan and heat gently, stirring occasionally until the mixture begins to steam. Whisk the egg yolks with the salt and sugar until pale. Gradually add the milk mixture to the egg yolks whilst constantly whisking and return to a low heat. Continue to stir until the mixture coats the back of a spoon. Allow to cool before putting in the fridge and leave overnight.

Place the mixture into an ice cream machine and allow to churn per manufacturer's instructions. Finley chop half the popcorn and cook gently in the butter. When the butter starts to foam and turn slightly brown, add to the ice cream. When the ice cream has almost frozen, add the remaining popcorn whole. Put into a freezer proof container and freeze.

For The Hazelnut Praline

Line a tray with baking parchment. Put the sugar into a heavy bottomed saucepan with the water and lemon juice and allow to caramelise over a medium heat. When the mixture is golden, add the nuts and quickly pour onto the baking sheet. Let it cool at room temperature before breaking into shards.

To Serve

Assemble as in picture with a swirl of black cherry purée.

110
KILLIECRANKIE HOTEL

Killiecrankie, By Pitlochry, Perthshire, PH16 5LG

01796 473 220
www.killiecrankiehotel.co.uk

The Killiecrankie Hotel stands at the head of the famous Pass of Killiecrankie, close to the site of the renowned Battle of Killiecrankie which marked the start of the first Jacobite uprising in 1689. Having recently been incorporated into the Cairngorms National Park, Killiecrankie is an ideal spot from which to base any sightseeing or walking tour of Scotland.

Owned by Henrietta Fergusson since 2007, this personally-run hotel continues to reach increasingly high standards. Always a popular spot, the hotel achieved The Good Hotel Guide César for Scottish Hotel of the Year, in addition to three red stars from the AA and three gold diamonds from Visit Scotland. Mark Easton has been awarded two AA rosettes for his food for the past 17 years – a remarkable achievement in itself. The wine list is comprehensive, so to help those not so sure of their wines, the daily changing menu carries suggestions of delicious wine to complement each dish.

Staying at The Killiecrankie Hotel is just like staying with friends. You are looked after by wonderful staff and you will find lots of extra touches, such as hot water bottles when you retire to bed, vegetables and flowers from the gardens and breakfast marmalade made by Henrietta's nonagenarian mother, who also provides the baking for Afternoon Tea!

Set in just under five acres of gardens and woodland, just minutes from the A9 and yet, so quiet The Killiecrankie provides a haven to which one can return after the rigours of a day's walk, the stress of catching that elusive salmon, or simply to relax after meandering through the spectacular Perthshire countryside.

Relish Restaurant Rewards
See page 003 for details.

Mark Easton has spent the past 17 years honing his skills (and indulging his passions) at Killiecrankie. He and his sous chef, Wayne Reeves, spend much of their time devising new recipes and trying fresh combinations - Mark's food is carefully sourced, as locally as possible, and closely scrutinised for quality at all times. For ingredients that have to come from further afield, he is discerning in his choice of suppliers.

SEARED KING SCALLOPS WITH A WARM FRENCH BEAN & CHORIZO TARTLET

SERVES 4

Albarino Veiga Naum, Rias Baixas 2010
(Spain)

Method

Sauté the chorizo with a little rapeseed oil then add beans to warm through.

Warm the puff pastry cases.

Sear the scallops in a very hot pan with rapeseed oil until golden brown. Season with smoked Maldon salt.

For The Herb Oil

Blanch herbs in boiling water for 20 seconds.

Plunge into icy water.

Squeeze out all the liquid. Liquidise with olive oil and store in fridge until required.

To Serve

Dress the plates with herb oil and place tartlets in centre. Divide the beans and chorizo between the tartlets, arranging any extra around the outside.

Place three scallops on each and spoon a small amount of cooking juice on each scallop.

Sprinkle micro herbs to garnish.

> **Chef's Tip**
> These days so many people prefer to steer clear of gluten in their diet – so simply omit the tartlet and add a few lightly dressed salad leaves.

Ingredients

12 king scallops
drizzle of rapeseed oil
smoked Maldon sea salt (to season)
100g *blanched* French beans (cut in half)
100g chorizo (halved and sliced)
4 x 7cm puff pastry cases

Herb Oil

25g each parsley and coriander
200ml olive oil

ROAST PERTHSHIRE LAMB WITH RED ONION MARMALADE MOUSSE

SERVES 4

 Fleurie, Hotel d'Aviron 2009 (France)

Ingredients

For The Lamb

300g best end Perthshire lamb (boned and trimmed)
175g lean minced lamb
50g red onion marmalade
4 slices Parma ham

Carrot Purée

150g carrots (peeled and sliced)
knob of butter

Potatoes

4 large Maris Piper potatoes
knob of butter

Kale

150g curly kale (washed, trimmed, shredded and *blanched*)
knob of butter

Madeira Jus

200ml lamb stock
40ml Madeira
seasoning

Method

For The Lamb

Mix together minced lamb and red onion marmalade. Roll out clingfilm one and a half times the length of lamb. Lay the Parma ham on the clingfilm, place the lamb on top and finally the mince and marmalade mix. Wrap the Parma ham around to enclose all together and use clingfilm to roll tightly into a sausage. Refrigerate for four to six hours.

Chef's Tip

Don't waste time preparing the lamb, ask your butcher to do it for you - he will be quicker and probably better!

For The Potatoes

Peel potatoes and use a 5cm cutter to cut into a cylinder. Melt butter in an ovenproof dish and add the potatoes. Season and cover with tinfoil and bake for 30 minutes at 180°C. After 30 minutes, remove the foil and continue baking for an additional 15 minutes.

For The Carrot Purée

Cook the carrots in a little water and butter until soft and then purée in a food processor and season.

To Cook The Lamb

Cut lamb into four equal portions. Place in an oiled non-stick ovenproof pan and roast for 14 minutes at 215°C then rest for ten minutes in a warm place.

For The Kale

Sauté curly kale with butter.

For The Madeira Jus

Flambé the Madeira, add stock then reduce by half.

To Serve

Place potato on the side of a warm plate. Slice the lamb and fan onto the plate. Add curly kale and a quenelle of carrot purée. Finish by spooning the Madeira *jus* over the lamb.

COCONUT, LIME & MALIBU PANNA COTTA

SERVES 4

*Casa Silva Semillon/Gewürztraminer Late Harvest
2010 (Chile)*

Ingredients

Panna Cotta

425ml coconut milk
50g caster sugar
30ml Malibu liqueur
3 leaves gelatine
2 limes (zest and juice)
4 medium sized *dariole* moulds

Coulis

1 ripe mango (peeled and sliced)
icing sugar

Garnish

16 raspberries
Amaretti biscuits
lime leaves

Method

Chef's Tip

A perfect dessert for guests with a dairy allergy who are
always served fresh fruit salad – and the rest of your guests
will love it too!!

For The Panna Cotta

Soak the three leaves of gelatine in cold water until soft.

Zest limes, then juice, keeping the peel and juice separate.

Pour coconut milk into a mixing bowl.

Warm the lime juice and sugar until the sugar dissolves. Add the
Malibu liqueur and the soaked gelatine to the coconut milk before
adding lime zest. Blend.

Refrigerate, removing every 30 minutes to stir well until the
mixture begins to set.

Divide between four *dariole* moulds or ramekins and chill until set
(four to six hours).

For The Mango Coulis

Make the mango coulis by blending the flesh in a food processor
(with a little icing sugar if required).

To Serve

Turn out the panna cottas onto a large plate. Spoon the coulis
along one side and garnish with raspberries, Amaretti biscuits and
lime leaves.

120
THE KITCHIN

78 Commercial Street, Edinburgh, Midlothian, EH6 6LX

0131 555 1755
www.thekitchin.com

Tom Kitchin opened Edinburgh restaurant, The Kitchin with wife Michaela in 2006 on Leith's stylish Waterfront. In January 2007, The Kitchin was awarded a Michelin star, making Tom the youngest ever Scottish chef proprietor to achieve one at the age of 29.

Since then, the restaurant and chef Tom have received nationwide recognition with a number of accolades and awards which have included Best UK Restaurant in the Square Meal Awards (2011) and Observer Food Monthly Restaurant of the Year (2010), Four AA Rosettes (2010), AA Wine Award Scotland (2010), number two in UK Top 100 Best Restaurants by Eat Out Magazine (2009), a Caterer & Hotelkeeper (Catey) award for 'UK Newcomer of the Year' (2008) and 'Restaurant of the Year, Scotland' at the AA Centenary Awards (2008) and most recently The Kitchin was named 'Best Restaurant' in Scotland at the prestigious National Restaurant Awards 2012.

Tom has continued to build his reputation for innovative cooking and The Kitchin's philosophy 'From Nature to Plate', is a true reflection of his passion for the finest, freshest Scottish seasonal produce.

Photography by Marc Millar

Tom's culinary CV extends from early training at the five star Gleneagles Hotel to experience garnered working with some of the world's most renowned chefs and restaurants. This includes Pierre Koffmann at the three Michelin-starred La Tante Claire, London, three Michelin-starred restaurant Guy Savoy in Paris and Alain Ducasse's Louis XV restaurant in Monte Carlo.

Tom's passion for produce, seasonality and cooking is almost fanatical and is reflected in his books *From Nature to Plate: Seasonal Recipes from The Kitchin* (2009) and *Kitchin Suppers* (2012).

ROCKPOOL

SERVES 4

🍷 *Albarino Martin Codax 2011 (Spain)*
Crisp, aromatic, dry white with grapefruity
character and hints of herbs and green apples

Ingredients

Tomato Consommé

25 ripe tomatoes (roughly chopped)
$^1/_2$ bunch basil
2 cloves garlic
a generous splash of olive oil
salt and pepper

Rockpool

You can use any combination of fish and shellfish for this recipe and I tend to use what comes in fresh that day, or what my suppliers recommend, but here are some suggestions for you to try:

olive oil
1 shallot
1 tbsp parsley (chopped)
50ml white wine
8 squat lobster tails
50g crab (freshly cooked)
4 oysters
2 razor clams
8 mussels
8 surf clams
50g squid
40g brown shrimp
20g keta salmon eggs
1 fillet mackerel (raw)
1 scallop
60g samphire
60g sea aster
60g sea plantain

Method

For The Tomato Consommé

Place all the ingredients in a mixing bowl and leave them to infuse for ten minutes.

Place the chopped tomatoes in the food blender and blend until puréed.

Take a muslin or a cheese cloth and lay in a bowl. Pour the tomato mixture onto the cloth and tie the four corners together with a piece of string. Tie the string to a shelf so that the cloth is hanging and place a bowl underneath to catch all the drips.

For The Rockpool

Heat a heavy bottomed pan and add some olive oil. Add the shellfish - the mussels and clams (razor clams and surf clams). Then, add the shallots, parsley and white wine and place a lid on the pan. The razor clams should be the first to open so, as they do, take them out of the pan.

Then, drop in the squid, squat lobster tails and brown shrimp and cook in the pan until warm.

Once the mussels and surf clams have opened, take them out of the pan and away from heat and remove from the shells.

Prepare the razor clams by removing the tender flash from the intestine.

Start to build the dish by dividing the shellfish between the four bowls. Then, add the cooked crab to the bowls evenly. Add a quarter slice of raw scallop, oysters and the salmon caviar.

Garnish with all your sea vegetables – samphire, sea aster and sea plantain.

To Serve

Pour the tomato consommé into a jug.

When you're serving the dish to your guests it's great to explain all the different ingredients you've used, and then pour the tomato consommé over each dish at the table - I always like to tell my guests that's like the tide coming in! A genuine re-creation of a rockpool!

Chef's Tip

Try and source as many different unusual seafood as you can get to make the dish as exciting as possible. Variations of seaweed also adds a special touch and flavour.

POACHED TURBOT WITH SAFFRON BROTH & SQUID INK PASTA

SERVES 4

🍷 *Chardonnay Coopers Creek Swamp Reserve 2009 (New Zealand)*
Big bold fruit driven Chardonnay with well integrated oak and grape intensity

Ingredients

4 pieces of turbot - roughly 150g each (or any poaching fish)
100ml fish stock
pinch saffron
100g fresh seaweed
30g unsalted butter
200g freshly podded broad beans (skinned)
1 tbsp whipping cream
1 tbsp tomato concasse
500g fresh squid ink pasta (from your local deli)
salt and pepper

Method

For The Turbot

Pour the 100ml fish stock in a fairly heavy bottomed pan and bring to a boil, then add a pinch of saffron. Lower the heat and simmer gently for two to three minutes.

Season the turbot on both sides and then place into the pan with the fish stock and poach gently for three to five minutes. Turn the turbot over and cook on the other side for four to five minutes. You can check if your turbot is cooked by gently inserting a needle into the thickest part of the flesh - if there is no resistance, it means the fish is cooked. When the turbot is ready, remove it from the pan and keep it warm.

> #### Chef's Tip
> I have made this recipe with turbot but it works just as well with monkfish or halibut.

For The Saffron Broth

Reduce the poaching *liquor* until it is reduced by three quarters, add the 30g of butter and tablespoon of whipping cream, then add the broad beans and simmer until tender.

For The Seaweed

Bring a saucepan of water to a boil and *blanch* the seaweed individually for three to four seconds.

For The Squid Ink Pasta

Cook according to instructions.

To Serve

Place the turbot on a plate and ladle the sauce over the fish, then garnish with the *blanched* seaweed and tomato concasse. Serve with squid ink spaghetti.

SUMMER STRAWBERRY MILLEFEUILLE

SERVES 4

 Coteaux du Layon 2010, Domaine des Baumard (France)
Delicate, light dessert wine with lovely scents of white flowers underpinned with a steely mineral character carrying a great freshness

Ingredients

Base

4 sheets ready made filo pastry
100ml *clarified butter*
100ml icing sugar

Caramel Tuile

200g caster sugar
crushed nuts or cracked black pepper (to taste)

Crowdie Mousse

500ml milk
vanilla of 1 pod (scrape the vanilla from the pod)
2 lemons (zest)
100g caster sugar
15g butter
30g cornflour
4 eggs
450g Crowdie cheese
200ml double cream
3 leaves of gelatine
400g fresh strawberries (sliced)

Garnish

400g fresh strawberries
fresh strawberry sorbet

Chef's Tip

Most berries in season are ideal for this recipe, so feel free to experiment and make the dish your own.

Method

For The Base

Preheat the oven to 180°C.

Place one sheet of filo pastry on a baking tray, and brush it with *clarified butter*, then sprinkle with icing sugar. Then, take your second sheet of filo pastry and repeat, placing one sheet on top of another until all four are brushed with butter, sprinkled with icing sugar and layered on top of one another.

Place the pastry onto a pastry mat or greaseproof paper. Layer another sheet of greaseproof paper on top, and then cover with another baking tray, so that your pastry is sandwiched inbetween.

Cook in the oven for six to eight minutes, until the pastry is golden brown. Take it out of the oven and quickly cut your desired shape - if you do this while it's still warm you will find it easier to cut your desired shape.

For The Caramel Tuile

This may seem a challenging part of the recipe but it's actually very simple.

Place 200g sugar into a heavy bottomed pan and heat gently until it forms and becomes golden all over. Remove from the heat and pour over a sheet of greaseproof paper on a baking tray and leave until the mixture goes hard.

Once the mixture is solid, place it in your blender – the mix will begin to form a caramel powder. Take a pastry mat and sprinkle the caramel powder thinly across it. Cut into the caramel with a cutter - you can choose any shape you wish and, if you prefer, you can also add nuts or cracked black pepper to taste. Very, very carefully, using a blow torch, blow torch the caramel and, as it heats, it will form a shape.

For The Crowdie Mousse

Place the Crowdie cheese, milk, vanilla, lemon zest, sugar, butter, cornflour and eggs into a thermal mix if you have one. Heat to 100°C and cook until the mix becomes thick.

If you don't have a thermal mix, you can put on a *bain-marie* or water bath. Put all of the ingredients together in a bowl. Place the bowl on top of the *bain-marie* and cook out slowly until all of the ingredients form a thick mixture. Set aside the Crowdie mixture and leave to chill.

Whip 195ml of cream – keep 5ml of cream back for later.

Meanwhile, soak three leaves of gelatine in cold water and place in a pan with the remaining 5ml cream and warm gently until the gelatine melts completely. Then, add in and fold the whipped cream and gelatine into the Crowdie mixture.

To Serve

Place a layer of the filo pastry on a plate. Cover the pastry with a layer of the Crowdie mousse, then a layer of sliced strawberries and repeat for all four layers. Once finished, place the caramel tuile on top and garnish with the Crowdie mousse, fresh strawberries and a fresh strawberry sorbet.

130
LIME TREE
AN EALDHAIN

Achintore Road, Fort William, PH33 6RQ

01397 701 806
www.limetreefortwilliam.co.uk

At the west end of Fort William High Street, overlooking Loch Linnhe and the mountains beyond, is the Lime Tree An Ealdhain - a former 1850 church Manse. It has been lovingly refurbished and expanded to create a stylish hotel, award-winning restaurant and high quality art gallery, capable of hosting exhibitions from touring national art collections.

The business gets its name from the old Lime Tree in the garden. 'An Ealdhain' is Gaelic, meaning 'the creative place'.

Visit the Lime Tree An Ealdhain and take the opportunity to relax in our Victorian lounges with their open fires or research your next day on the hills in our map room. Our restaurant is open plan so you will see, hear and more importantly be able to enjoy the aroma of your meal being prepared for you.

The Lime Tree An Ealdhain restaurant ethos is that our food should be made from fresh, seasonal/raw ingredients sourced locally where possible. Head chef William MacDonald, sous Graham Stuchbury and the team then use their skills as talented young chefs to create dishes with a strong Scottish identity.

Together with comfortable, stylish and individual accommodation, the Lime Tree is a place to relax and to feel at home in the heart of the Highlands.

Lime Tree An Ealdhain gets its name from the 200-year-old Lime Tree found in the garden and 'an Ealdhain' is Gaelic meaning 'the creative place'.

PAN SEARED HAUNCH OF VENISON, POTATO & CHESTNUT DUMPLING, TEXTURES OF PEAR & PARSLEY ROOT PUREE, JUNIPER BERRY JUS

SERVES 6

 Chianti/Primitivo (Italy)

Ingredients

For The Venison

300g best end venison haunch
300ml red cooking wine
1 tbsp (10) peppercorns
3 tbsp juniper berries
1 tbsp star anise
3 bay leaves
15ml vegetable oil

Potato And Chestnut Dumpling

900g potatoes
2 eggs
300g plain flour
40g chestnuts

Parsley Root Purée

200g parsley root
500ml vegetable stock
25g butter
50ml double cream

Juniper Berry Jus

400ml beef demi-glaze
2 tbsp red wine
1 tbsp red wine vinegar
2 tbsp juniper berries
300ml red wine marinade (reserved from the venison marinade)

Pear

2 large whole pears (still firm)
30ml pear juice (apple juice can be used as an alternative)

Method

For The Venison

Trim the venison and divide into roughly 50g portions. Mix other ingredients and bring to a boil. Simmer for ten to 15 minutes and allow to cool slightly. Strain marinade through sieve and cover venison with it. Allow to stand for one to two hours. This can be done the day before. Retain the marinade for sauce.

For The Potato And Chestnut Dumpling

Peel and cook the potatoes. Mash potatoes, mix in beaten egg and sieve in flour. Mix to combine. Roughly chop chestnuts and roast for ten minutes at 180°C. Blitz roughly in food processor and add to potatoes. Season well. Line 30cm by 15cm tin with greaseproof, pour in potato mix and spread evenly. Sit tin in larger tin half full of water, cover with tinfoil and bake at 150°C for one hour. Allow to cool and divide into portions.

For The Parsley Root Purée

Peel and finely chop parsley root. Add to stock and butter. Boil until tender. Blend with hand blender, adding cream until a smooth, light purée forms. Pass through fine sieve and season to taste.

For The Juniper Berry Jus

Reduce demi-glaze by half. Reduce wine and juniper to light syrup and add stock. Simmer, reducing until coating back of spoon. Strain and add two tablespoons of wine and one tablespoon vinegar, then season to taste. Keep warm until ready to serve.

For The Pear

Peel and finely chop one pear. Heat gently with the pear juice in a small pan until the pear is soft. Blend using a hand blender and pass through a fine sieve. Peel and finely dice the other pear. Set aside until required.

To Serve

Warm the dumpling through in the oven for ten minutes (180°C). Heat a small pan with the vegetable oil over a high heat. Add the venison, reduce to a medium heat and cook the meat to your preference. Set aside in a warm place and allow to rest for two to three minutes. Slice the venison and assemble the dish as pictured. Garnish with diced pear and *jus*.

BALLOTINE MONKFISH WRAPPED IN SMOKED SALMON WITH LEMON SCENTED CRUSHED VIOLET POTATOES, PANFRIED SAMPHIRE, MUSSELS & A SHELLFISH VELOUTE

SERVES 6

🍷 *Riesling (Germany)*
🍷 *Pinot Noir (New Zealand)*

Ingredients

Monkfish
900g (6 x 150g) monkfish
200g sliced smoked salmon

Potatoes
1kg violet potatoes
25g unsalted butter
1 lemon (zest and juice)

Samphire
300g samphire
25g unsalted butter

Mussels
1kg mussels
200ml white wine
2 cloves garlic
1 onion
20g dill
olive oil

Mussels
100ml double cream
juice from mussels

Method

For The Monkfish
Wrap monkfish in smoked salmon, roll tightly in clingfilm and twist ends. Refrigerate until required.

For The Violet Potatoes
Boil violet potatoes. Once cooked, run under cold water to cool. When cooled, peel and crush into small pieces. Put 25g of butter in a hot pan with the zest and juice of the lemon. Add the violet potatoes and turn down heat. Leave to warm through for three to four minutes and season to taste.

For The Samphire
Blanch samphire in boiling water for about 30 seconds then drain. Put 25g of butter into a hot pan, add samphire, mix well, set aside and keep warm.

For The Mussels
Chop onion, garlic and dill and panfry with the olive oil until opaque. Add wine and bring to a boil. Add mussels and cover with the lid for two to three minutes or until all mussels have opened. Discard any unopened mussels, drain the juice and keep aside. Set mussels aside and keep warm.

For The Velouté
Bring the juice from the mussels back to a boil, add the double cream and reduce by one third.

To Serve
Put a pan of boiling water on high heat to poach the monkfish for about eight to ten minutes.

Slice the monkfish into portions then assemble dish as pictured. Garnish with small sprigs of dill.

Chef's Tip
When slicing the ballotine, slice one end right through and then remove the clingfilm. This will help keep the smoked salmon and monkfish in one piece.

TRIPLE CHOCOLATE & WHISKY BAVAROIS WITH BUTTERSCOTCH SAUCE, CRANACHAN ICE CREAM & CANDIED HAZELNUTS

SERVES 6

🍷 *Muscat (France)*
🍷 *Shiraz (South East Australia)*

Ingredients

Bavarois

5 egg yolks
25g caster sugar, 165ml milk
4 sheets gelatine
75g white chocolate
75g milk chocolate
75g dark chocolate
360ml double cream (lightly whipped)
75ml whisky

Butterscotch Sauce

150g dark sugar
200ml double cream
30g butter

Cranachan Ice Cream

100ml cream, 250ml milk
30ml honey
30g caster sugar
3 egg yolks
40g pinhead oats (toasted)
25ml whisky

Candied Hazelnuts

50g hazelnuts (toasted)
100g caster sugar

Method

For The Bavarois

Line loaf tin with clingfilm. Soak gelatine leaves in cold water. Whisk egg yolks and sugar until pale and fluffy. Heat milk, remove from heat and whisk in gelatine. Pour milk mix over egg mix, whisking continuously. Return mix to low heat, whisking until thick - careful not to scramble the eggs. Put chocolate in separate bowls and add 25ml of whisky to each. Divide egg mix equally between the three bowls and stir until chocolate is dissolved. Fold in the cream. Pour the white chocolate mix into the loaf tin and refrigerate for 30 minutes. Pour on milk chocolate and refrigerate for a further 30 minutes. Pour on dark chocolate and refrigerate for a minimum of one hour to set.

> **Chef's Tip**
> Whilst each layer is chilling, the remaining mixes must be kept in a warm place to prevent them from setting.

For The Butterscotch Sauce

Place all ingredients in a pan on low/medium heat until combined and caramel in colour.

For The Cranachan Ice Cream

Heat milk, honey and cream together. Whisk egg yolks and sugar until pale and fluffy. Pour over cream mix, whisking continuously. Return mix to low heat and whisk until thicker (approximately five minutes). Place mix in ice cream machine and churn until almost set. Toast off oats in a pan on low heat. Add oats and whisky to ice cream and re-churn until done. Transfer to the freezer.

For The Candied Hazelnuts

Toast hazelnuts in a pan on low heat. Place sugar in a pan on medium heat until the sugar has melted and is caramel in colour, watching that it doesn't darken too much. Place nuts on greaseproof paper and pour caramel over them. Leave to cool then break apart with sharp knife.

To Serve

Slice the bavarois into portions using a hot knife and assemble as pictured.

140
LOCH NESS INN

Lewiston, Drumnadrochit, Inverness-shire, IV63 6UW

01456 450 991
www.staylochness.co.uk

Once home to a brewery, the Loch Ness Inn is an atmospheric, friendly inn tucked away in Lewiston, just south of Drumnadrochit. Regularly winning awards for its warm welcome and outstanding food, it is ideal for those wishing to explore Loch Ness, visit nearby Urquhart Castle or walk the Great Glen Way, which passes the doorstep.

Head chef Debbie Carr's menu showcases the wonderful regional ingredients - west coast fish, Highland beef, lamb and venison. Debbie used to run the kitchen at the Applecross Inn, the Loch Ness's sister establishment, and also serves Applecross Bay prawns, brought straight from Applecross. Both inns, overseen by Judith Fish, pride themselves on locally sourced good food and Highland hospitality.

The building was recently renovated, restoring much of its original 1830's character. Taking its inspiration from lochs and glens, the interior, including 12 individually designed bedrooms, is decorated with Highland tweeds and pastel colours. In summer, a secluded courtyard at the rear of the Inn, overlooking the River Coaltie, provides an outdoor dining area and the restaurant welcomes winter visitors with a double-fronted wood-burning stove.

The Brewery Bar serves ales from the Loch Ness Brewery, including the Inn's own 'Inn-dige-Ness', plus a fine wine list and range of malts. The bar is the base for this year's Macaulay Cup winners, Glen Urquhart Shinty Team, so expect a lively atmosphere!

Relish Restaurant Rewards
See page 003 for details.

Awarded Real & Local Food 2012 and Rising Star Inn 2011, the Inn appears in the Michelin Guide. All this stems from local girl Isla Urquhart, who won Rising Star Hospitality Manager of the Year. She brings the whole place together and has developed the business in many directions.

WARM GOAT'S CHEESE TOPPED WITH LOCAL HONEY & ALMONDS WITH HOMEMADE TAPENADE

SERVES 4

 Old Coach Road, Sauvignon Blanc (New Zealand)

Method

For The Tapenade

Chop the tomatoes and olives into very small pieces. Mix with the olive oil.

Finely chop the lemon zest. Mix the chopped zest and chopped parsley into the olive and tomato mixture.

For The Goat's Cheese, Honey And Almonds

Place the almonds on a baking sheet and grill gently until golden. Lightly grease a baking tray and place the goat's cheese slices on it. Grill until golden.

Sprinkle the almonds over the goat's cheese and drizzle about a dessert spoon of honey over each slice. Warm through in a low oven.

Chef's Tip

Take care not to over-brown the almonds as they will become bitter.

To Serve

Dress the plate with the mixed leaves and the tapenade. Carefully place the goat's cheese on top of the leaves. Serve immediately.

Ingredients

Goat's Cheese

25g flaked almonds
4 slices hard goat's cheese (1-1¹/₂ cm thick)
4 dtsp runny honey

Tapenade

25g sundried tomatoes
25g pitted black olives
10ml olive oil
¹/₂ lemon (zest)
4 sprigs parsley (leaves picked and finely chopped)

Garnish

mixed salad leaves

Squat Lobsters

SEAFOOD LINGUINI

SERVES 4

Marques de Caceres Rioja Blanco
(Spain)

Ingredients

Pasta

600g linguini
10ml olive oil
1 tsp salt

Sauce

1 red pepper
15 cherry tomatoes
olive oil
8 to 12 scallops (rinsed and patted dry)
2 smoked haddock fillets (cut into 3 or 4cm pieces)
200g shelled cooked mussels
40ml double cream
50g rocket

Garnish

peashoots

Method

The Loch Ness Inn gets exceptional seafood from the west coast of Scotland. This popular dish makes great use of fresh scallops.

For The Pasta

Bring a large pan of water to a boil. Add the oil and the salt. Place the linguini in the water and stir frequently for the first two minutes. Simmer for 15 to 20 minutes or until soft.

Meanwhile, prepare the sauce.

For The Sauce

Dice the pepper into 1cm pieces. Halve the tomatoes. Heat a little oil in a frying pan and add the pepper. Fry gently until soft. Add the tomatoes and cook for a further minute. Set aside.

In a large frying pan, heat a little olive oil until very hot and carefully add the scallops to the pan. Cook on a high heat for two to three minutes until golden brown on both sides.

Reduce the heat to low. Add the haddock, mussels and the tomato and pepper mix. Stir and cook for a minute or two. Pour in half the cream and bring to a boil. Use the other half only if needed.

Add in the rocket, give everything a good stir and remove from the heat. Adjust the seasoning.

Chef's Tip

Make sure that you dry the scallops, and remove the pan from the direct heat when adding to pan. Take care - they can spit!

To Serve

Drain the cooked pasta and season with salt and pepper. Place into warmed serving bowls. Pour the sauce over. Sprinkle peashoots over each dish and serve.

LEMON POSSET WITH BRANDY SNAP FINGERS

SERVES 4 - 6

🍷 *A good quality Riesling, sweet and acidic,
or Edinburgh Raspberry Infused Gin (quirky
and Scottish)*

Ingredients

Lemon Posset

1.2 ltr double cream
300g caster sugar
4 lemons (juice of)
1 punnet Scottish raspberries (optional)

Brandy Snaps

25g butter
25g demerara sugar
25g golden syrup
25g plain flour
10ml brandy
$^1/_2$ tsp ground ginger

Garnish

icing sugar (for dusting)

Method

Lemon posset is one of those traditional desserts that are very difficult to resist!

Lemon Posset

Place the cream, sugar and lemon juice in a pan and boil for three minutes.

Pour the lemon posset mix in a wine glass or small bowl and allow to set for a few hours in the fridge.

As an option, place four to six raspberries in the bottom of the glass or bowl.

Brandy Snaps

Heat the butter, sugar and golden syrup in a pan until boiling. Remove from the heat.

Stir in the flour, brandy and ground ginger. Mix until combined.

Let the mixture sit for a few minutes. Meanwhile, preheat the oven to 160°C.

Put teaspoon-sized balls of mixture onto a greaseproof sheet or silicone mat, making sure they are not too close together - they will spread! Cook in the oven until golden, approximately seven to ten minutes.

Remove from the oven and allow to cool slightly but not set.

While they are still pliable, wrap each brandy snap around the handle of a wooden spoon before leaving on a greaseproof sheet to set.

Dust with icing sugar and serve with the posset.

Chef's Tip

If the brandy snaps are too hard you can warm in the oven. Allow to cool.

To Serve

Serve as pictured.

150
NICK NAIRN
COOK SCHOOL

Port of Menteith, Stirling, FK8 3JZ

01877 389 900
www.nairnscookschool.com

I started the Cook School with a very simple aim - to help people learn to cook. Each class we teach gives cooks of all levels extra confidence, actual skills and a day out full of chat, cooking, eating and drinking. I never get tired of seeing people, who started the day a bit unsure, leave after a few hours beaming and unable to believe what fantastic food they've created.

We're lucky to have a top team of tutors at both our Cook Schools - here in the heart of the Trossachs at Port of Menteith and at our newer central Aberdeen school. In fact our main man, chef tutor John Webber, is so good he recently won the British Cookery Schools UK Tutor of the Year award. Customers' words of praise for John practically filled our entire facebook page. He is about the most modest person on the planet so he won't shout about it - but I will! There aren't many people who have so many useful facts and tips (and bad jokes) at their fingertips as John. He is a star.

In Port of Menteith we run mostly full day classes, though there are also three hour 'Skills' sessions. Up in Aberdeen, we run full days as well as 'Quick Cooks' which are just two hours - great for after work, a weekend morning or an extended lunch hour. On these you learn to cook one delicious dish, plus all sorts of cheffy tips (chopping, sauces, etc), and of course you get to eat what you've made, with a glass of wine if you fancy.

Hope to see you at a class soon xx *Nick Nairn*

For class information at both Nick Nairn cook schools, including prices, booking and gift cards, plus recipes, online shop and general foodie gossip, head for www.nicknairn.com

We're so lucky in Scotland to have such wonderful natural produce as freshly dived scallops, fabulous fish and an abundance of expertly reared meat. These are just some of the fantastic ingredients we use at both Cook Schools.

I hope you enjoy my dinner party style meal here - nothing in it is too difficult to make. It's really all about great ingredients and getting prepared ahead of time. And if shucking scallops puts the fear into you, come on my 'New Scottish Cookery' course here at the Cook School and I'll turn you into a master shucker in no time!

SEARED SCALLOP & BLACK PUDDING SALAD WITH CRISPY PANCETTA

SERVES 4

Vouvray 'Cuvee Silex', Vigneau Chevreau,
Loire Valley (France)

Ingredients

Scallops

8 hand-dived king scallops (freshly *shucked*)
sunflower oil
$^1/_2$ lemon (juice)
4 slices Stornoway black pudding
8 slices pancetta
Maldon sea salt
freshly milled black pepper

Salad And Dressing

150g mixed organic salad leaves
20g picked herbs (flat parsley, dill, coriander)
5ml lemon juice
20ml extra virgin olive oil
4 tbsp crème fraîche

Method

For The Scallops

It's best to *shuck* the scallops yourself. Come to the Cook School and we'll teach you how! Otherwise ask the fishmonger to do it and cook as soon as possible afterwards.

Preheat the oven to 200°C. Lay the slices of pancetta on to a baking-paper lined tray and cook in the oven until crisp. Remove, but leave the oven on.

Heat a griddle pan until fairly hot. Brush the scallops with sunflower oil and a little clear fat from the pancetta tray.

Place four oiled scallops into the hot griddle pan and sprinkle with a little salt and a small squeeze of lemon. Cook for a minute, then, using tongs, turn them 90°C and leave for another minute, so you end up with a criss-cross pattern from the griddle pan on each scallop. Turn them over and repeat. Total cooking time four minutes. Place on a warm tray while you cook the rest.

Reheat the pan and remove the skin from the black pudding slices. Brush with oil and cook for a minute or two on both sides.

To Serve

Mix the lemon juice and olive oil and toss the leaves and herbs in a little of this dressing.

Warm through the tray of scallops and black pudding in the oven for no more than one minute. Grind over a little pepper.

Plate as pictured. Stir the crème fraîche and run a little off a teaspoon around each plate. Drizzle around a little more salad dressing and serve immediately.

Food photography by Paul Dodds

CRISPY SEA BASS WITH CELERIAC REMOULADE, SUNBLUSHED TOMATO SALSA & TAPENADE

SERVES 4

 Domus By Domaine d'Uby
(France)

Ingredients

Sea Bass

4 fillets sea bass
25g unsalted butter
splash olive oil
Maldon salt
freshly ground black pepper
lemon (squeeze of)

Tapenade

25g tinned anchovies
100g pitted black olives
1 tbsp mini salted capers (rinsed and drained)
1 garlic clove (minced)
150ml good olive oil
Maldon salt
freshly ground black pepper

Celeriac Remoulade

1/2 peeled celeriac
1 tsp good quality grain mustard
2 tbsp mayonnaise (Hellmann's is fine)
Maldon salt
freshly ground black pepper
lemon (squeeze of)

Salsa

80g sunblushed tomatoes in oil (halved)
120g cherry tomatoes (halved)
1 shallot (finely chopped)
6 basil leaves (torn)
100ml good olive oil
Maldon salt
freshly ground black pepper
30ml best Cabernet Sauvignon vinegar (we use
Forum, available at www.nicknairn.com)

Method

For The Tapenade

Take all the ingredients apart from the oil and blend until smooth. Season, then add the oil. The texture should be thick.

For The Celeriac Remoulade

Finely slice the celeriac, preferably with a mandolin, and shred finely with a very sharp knife. Stir in the mayonnaise, mustard and lemon juice. Season to taste. Cover and refrigerate.

For The Salsa

Mix all the tomatoes with the shallot. Season and add olive oil. Leave to marinate and add the basil just before serving.

For The Sea Bass

Take a heavy bottomed frying pan and place on the heat. Add the oil, heat for five seconds and add the fish, skin side down. Leave the fish long enough to let the natural sugars form a caramelised crust. When you see a golden brown edge, gently turn it and allow the pan to cool slightly. Add the butter and a squeeze of lemon and remove to a warm area to rest for a minute.

To Serve

Place a round mousse ring on a plate and spoon in your remoulade. Leave to settle for ten seconds then remove the ring. Place the warm fish on top. Use two dessert spoons to shape a neat helping of the tapenade on top of the fish. Spoon around the chunky tomato salsa and drizzle around any leftover tapenade oil.

Chef's Tip

All accompaniments can be made ahead so, at the time, just cook the fish and plate up.

Food photography by Paul Dodds

CLOTTED CREAM PANNA COTTA WITH GRENADINE RHUBARB & A TUILE TWIST

SERVES 4

🍷 *Oremus Tokaji Late Harvest Sweet Furmint Halves (Hungary)*

Ingredients

Panna Cotta

250g clotted cream (not with a butter crust)
150ml full fat milk
1 1/4 leaves gelatine (soaked in cold water for 5 minutes)
1 vanilla pod (split, seeds removed)
25g caster sugar

Tuile

50g icing sugar
50g soft butter
50g plain flour
50g egg white (unbeaten - just under 2 eggs, but do measure it)

Rhubarb

100g caster sugar
50ml water
50ml grenadine syrup
100g rhubarb (cut thinly on a sharp angle)

Garnish

4 mint sprigs

Method

For The Panna Cotta

Place the vanilla pod and seeds into a pan with the milk and sugar. Bring to a boil, remove from the heat.

Place the clotted cream into a bowl and stir to soften.

When infused, bring the milk pan back to a boil and add the gelatine. Turn off the heat. Allow the gelatine to dissolve. Cool thoroughly or the heat will make the clotted cream grainy. Pour through a sieve into the clotted cream and fold in. Place the bowl over ice and refrigerate until just starting to set.

Remove from the fridge and stir to redistribute the vanilla seeds. Divide between glasses or moulds and refrigerate for at least four hours. The final texture should be firm but creamy, not blancmangey.

For The Tuiles

Heat the oven to 180°C. Cream the butter and sugar. Add the flour and beat in. Add the egg white and mix thoroughly. Spread onto a stencil of a 10cm diameter circle on a lined baking tray. Fit two circles on the tray. Place into the oven for four minutes until the tuiles are just golden brown. Remove and shape each soft biscuit around a rolling pin making half tubes, then leave to cool. Repeat for two more.

For The Rhubarb

In a pan, bring the sugar, water and grenadine syrup to a boil. Add the rhubarb and simmer for a minute. Remove with a slotted spoon. Continue to reduce the syrup then leave. Once cooled, dip the rhubarb back into the cool syrup to intensify the flavour and hold the shape.

To Serve

When your panna cottas are ready, carefully invert onto cold dessert plates and serve as pictured.

> **Chef's Tip**
> If they won't unmould, dip each base briefly in warm water.

Food photography by Paul Dodds

160
THE PEAT INN

Cupar, Fife, KY15 5LH

01334 840 206
www.thepeatinn.co.uk

Situated seven miles outside St Andrews, The Peat Inn, first established in the 1700s, is a renowned restaurant with rooms, owned and run by Geoffrey and Katherine Smeddle.

Geoffrey is at the heart of the kitchen and Katherine's talents lie in her warmth and elegance front of house. With their very personal touch and expertise, they have achieved many accolades during their time at the inn, including a Michelin star. The eight individually designed suites in The Residence provide the perfect opportunity for a night away, where the pleasures of the table spill over into a charming overnight setting.

The restaurant is situated in the oldest part of the building with an open log fire to welcome you in the cold and dark winter months. Whilst there are some unmistakably modern touches, the elegant interior and intimate atmosphere create a dining experience which is rooted in classic values.

Based on values of warm personal service, fine cooking, an award winning wine list and relaxed ambiance, The Peat Inn continues to offer guests a delightful experience.

Relish Restaurant Rewards
See page 003 for details.

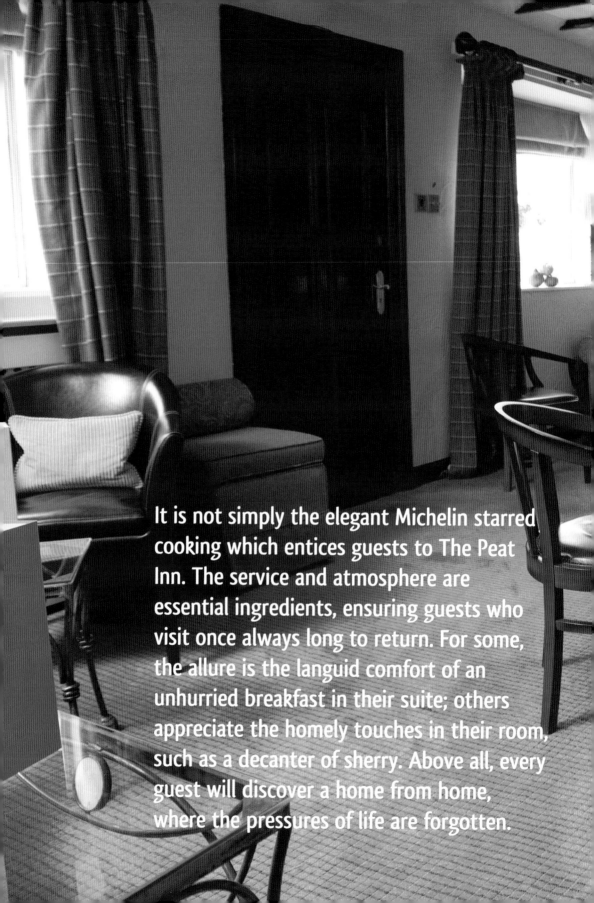

It is not simply the elegant Michelin starred cooking which entices guests to The Peat Inn. The service and atmosphere are essential ingredients, ensuring guests who visit once always long to return. For some, the allure is the languid comfort of an unhurried breakfast in their suite; others appreciate the homely touches in their room, such as a decanter of sherry. Above all, every guest will discover a home from home, where the pressures of life are forgotten.

OYSTER PANNA COTTA, BEETROOT CURED SALMON, DRESSED CRAB & AVOCADO CRÈME FRAICHE

SERVES 4

 The Old Block Semillon, Glenguin Estate,
New South Wales 2007 (Australia)

Ingredients

Oyster Panna Cotta

9 oysters (*shucked*, juice reserved)
1 banana shallot (finely diced)
60ml white wine
50ml milk
30ml of warm milk (for dissolving gelatine)
50ml double cream
30g unsalted butter
2 stems tarragon (chopped)
2 leaves gelatine (softened in iced water, then excess water squeezed out - ready to dissolve in the milk)

Salmon

$1/2$ a side of salmon (scaled, skin on, pin bones removed)
2 small heads raw beetroot (peeled)
1 lime (juice)
40g Maldon sea salt flakes
40g sugar

Crab

150g fresh white picked crab meat (all bone and shell removed), 1 dtsp chives (finely chopped), olive oil, lemon juice (to season) combine these ingredients to make dressed crab

Avocado Crème Fraiche

1 ripe avocado (flesh of)
1 dtsp good quality crème fraiche
lemon juice, salt

Shallots In Vinegar

4 banana shallots (very finely diced)
400ml sherry vinegar

To Decorate And Finish

caviar, fronds of chervil, micro herbs

Method

For The Panna Cotta

Melt the butter and sweat the shallot without colouring, add the tarragon and wine and reduce until almost evaporated. Add the cream and 50ml of milk and once it simmers, add the oysters and juice and cook for one minute. Blend thoroughly and press through a fine sieve.

Heat the 30ml of milk and dissolve the gelatine, then add this to the oyster base. Pour into a 17cm x 17cm square mould sprayed with spray wax, then base line tightly with clingfilm so it will hold the liquid as it sets without leaking. Chill on a flat tray until set, at least five hours. Carefully remove the mould and cut the panna cotta into fingers of your desired shape and size.

For The Salmon (Prepare the day before)

Place all the ingredients, apart from the salmon, in a food processor and blitz to a coarse pulp. Line a tray with double width clingfilm and layer with half the beetroot mix. Place the salmon on top, in the same direction, then cover it with the rest of the beetroot mixture. Wrap with clingfilm securely so that a minimal amount of juice can escape.

Refrigerate for 24 hours, turning once half way through. Once cured, rinse thoroughly under cold water then remove the skin. Cut into small cubes, then set aside.

For The Avocado Crème Fraiche

Blitz ingredients then add crème fraiche. Cover the surface of the purée with clingfilm to protect from oxidisation, then refrigerate for up to two hours.

For The Shallots

Place the banana shallot dice in a small saucepan and add 400ml sherry vinegar. Bring to a boil then simmer to reduce until all the liquid has evaporated leaving a moist compôte.

To Dress And Serve

Lift a portion of panna cotta onto the serving dish with a small palette knife. Spoon caviar and chervil leaves over the panna cotta. Swipe the avocado purée then arrange the crab meat and the cubes of salmon. Garnish with more herbs and a spoonful of the vinegar-shallot mixture. Enjoy!

SLOW BRAISED SHORT RIB OF SCOTCH BEEF, SMOKED BUTTERNUT SQUASH PUREE, GLAZED SHALLOTS, FONDANT CARROTS & RED WINE JUS

SERVES 4

 Ninquen, Ninquen Mountain Vineyard,
Colchagua Valley (Chile)

Ingredients

Beef
1 beef short rib (trimmed of excess fat)
1 carrot (peeled and sliced into thin coins)
1 onion (peeled and finely sliced)
1 rib of celery (sliced thinly)
1 head of garlic (cut in half across the face of the cloves)
500ml red wine
150ml ruby port
1 ltr brown chicken stock (to cover)
thyme and rosemary (generous sprigs)
1 bay leaf
salt and black pepper
1 spoonful redcurrant jelly

Butternut Squash Purée
1 butternut squash (peeled and seeds removed)
knob of butter
a scant amount of milk (to cover)
salt and pepper
sprig thyme
1 bay leaf

Glazed Shallots
4 large banana shallots (cut in half lengthways keeping roots in tact)
knob of butter
sprig thyme
300ml chicken stock

Fondant Carrots
4 large carrots (peeled and cut into 4 lengthways and shape with a swivel head peeler)
knob of butter
1 orange (juice)
pinch of sugar
water (to cover)
1 star anise, tarragon

Method

For The Beef
In a large saucepan, heat a film of vegetable oil and fry the garlic until gold. Add the thyme, bay leaf and rosemary and fry for one minute, then add the carrots. Fry for ten minutes, stirring regularly, then add the onion, celery and fry for five minutes. Add the wine and port, bring to a boil then simmer to reduce to compôte consistency.

Place the beef on top of the vegetables then add the stock so the meat is generously covered to allow for evaporation. Bring to a boil and cover with a greaseproof paper disc and then a lid. Cook at 130°C until the beef is tender, about two and a half hours.

Remove from the oven and stand for one hour to cool. Carefully remove the meat from the pot and transfer to a tray. Once cool, cut into fingers, allowing two per portion. Pass the cooking liquid through a fine sieve and set aside. Store the beef in this liquid.

For The Butternut Squash Purée
Slice the squash into pieces 1cm thick then arrange on a smoker tray. Smoke for eight minutes. Cut into smaller cubes and place in a heated saucepan with olive oil. Season with salt and pepper and sweat for ten minutes so it starts to break down and soften. Half cover with milk and add the thyme and bay leaf. Simmer until soft, strain through a sieve, collecting the milk in a bowl at the same time. Transfer the flesh to a mixer, discard the thyme and bay leaf and add just enough of the cooking milk to the blender to help it process to a purée. Add a knob of butter then taste for seasoning and set aside.

For The Carrots
Bring the carrots to a gentle simmer in the ingredients until soft and tender. Reheat in this liquid and serve with tarragon.

For The Glazed Shallots
Heat a cast iron frying pan and add some oil and the thyme then fry the shallots, cut side down, so the face turns a light gold. Add the stock and bring to a simmer. Transfer the pan to a preheated oven at 180°C until tender and the stock mostly absorbed. Transfer the shallots onto a tray, remove the skin and set aside.

To Serve
Heat the meat carefully in its *liquor*. Heat the shallots in the oven and warm the purée. Plate as in picture, decorate with wedges of roast butternut squash, then spoon some of the braising juices over the meat .

CHOCOLATE MOELLEUX, COCONUT MOUSSE & PASSION FRUIT

SERVES 4

 Rutherglen Muscat, Amber Gold, Campbell Brothers (Australia)

Ingredients

Chocolate Moelleux

125ml milk
125ml double cream
40g egg yolk
30g caster sugar
65g dark chocolate (broken into small pieces)

Coconut Mousse

1 1/2 leaves of gelatine (softened in iced water)
250g coconut purée
1 large egg white
30g caster sugar
75g double cream
75g Malibu
dash of cream (to heat to dissolve gelatine)

Chocolate Sable Biscuit Base

300g plain flour
30g dark cocoa powder
225g cold butter (cut into small cubes)
85g caster sugar
1 egg yolk

To Serve

pulp and seeds from a passion fruit
melted chocolate (to brush on the plate)

Method

For The Biscuit Base

Place all the ingredients, except for the egg, in a mixer and pulse to make a breadcrumb texture then transfer to a bowl and work in the egg by hand to bring the dough together. Form a couple of long batons of the dough, wrap in clingfilm then chill for at least two hours. After this time, roll out to a thickness of 3mm and cut bases measuring 8cm x 4cm. You need one per portion. Freeze any excess. Rest for two hours before baking on parchment paper at 180°C so the biscuit base sets to a dry crumbly pastry. Cool then store in an airtight container.

For The Chocolate Moelleux (Make the day before)

Make an anglaise - combine the milk and cream in a saucepan and bring almost to a boil. Meanwhile, combine the egg and sugar in a bowl and whisk together. Pour the milk and cream over the egg mix, stir well then return to the saucepan. Cook, stirring steadily to thicken, taking care not to scramble the mix. Once thickened, pour over the chocolate and stir to melt and mix. Cool slightly then transfer to a piping bag fitted with a 1cm plain nozzle. Refrigerate for 24 hours.

For The Coconut Mousse

Heat the coconut purée and simmer to reduce to give 150g. Stir in Malibu then cool. In a bowl, whip the egg white to a soft peak, gradually adding the sugar as you whisk. In another bowl, whip the cream to a firm peak. Heat the remaining cream and dissolve the gelatine in it, making sure to squeeze out excess water from the gelatine first, then stir into the coconut purée. Fold a quarter of the egg white into the coconut purée then a quarter of the cream, continue in turns until all are mixed into the base evenly. Set in tray lines with clingfilm and chill for six hours.

To Serve

Pipe straight lines of chocolate onto the sable biscuit base. Cut the coconut mousse into pieces measuring 8cm x 4cm and arrange on top of the piped chocolate. Lift onto the left hand side of a serving plate. Brush some melted chocolate down the right hand side of the plate and scatter some passion fruit pulp along it. Place a small scoop of coconut sorbet on the passion fruit then serve at once.

170 PURSLANE

33a St Stephen Street, Stockbridge, Edinburgh, EH3 5AH

0131 226 3500
www.purslanerestaurant.co.uk

Based in the stunning area of Stockbridge on St Stephen Street, this fantastic new restaurant is the epitome of rustic 'casual fine dining'. The restaurant does not dictate a dress code or formality; they want the customer to feel relaxed at all times.

The food assumes all fine dining elements, showcasing local produce with a mix of old and new techniques using worldwide influences.

Paul Gunning is at the helm of Purslane. Paul has experience working with chefs like Marco Pierre White (River Room MPW), Jeff Bland (Balmoral, Number 1), Phil Thompson (Auberge Du Lac) and Jean Michel Gauffre (La Garrigue).

The team feel strongly about the seasonality of the ingredients that are used to ensure the best quality. Most of their ingredients are sourced locally from suppliers based in the Stockbridge area. Some fantastic feedback is available to see on their website.

Paul looks forward to seeing you at Purslane for some relaxed casual fine dining!

Relish Restaurant Rewards
See page 003 for details.

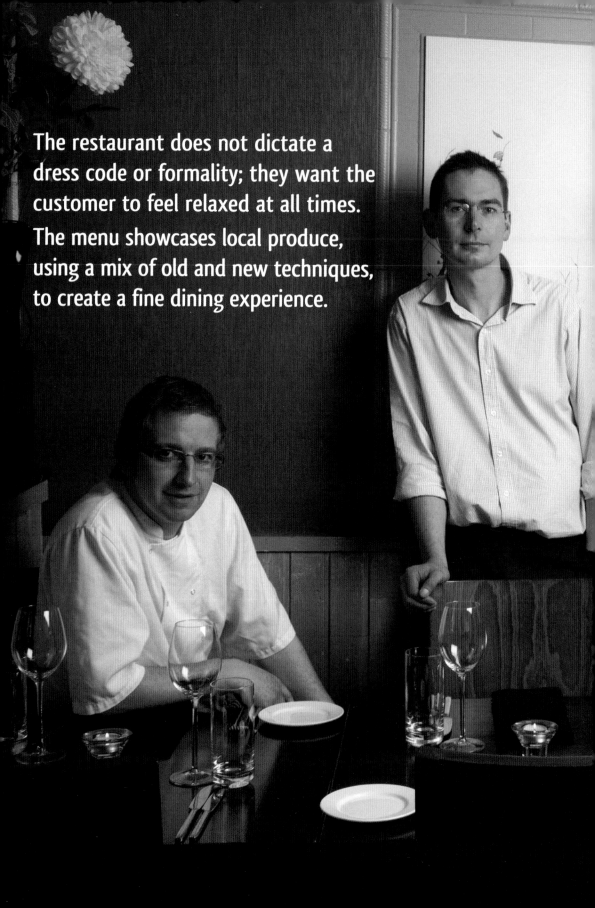

The restaurant does not dictate a dress code or formality; they want the customer to feel relaxed at all times. The menu showcases local produce, using a mix of old and new techniques, to create a fine dining experience.

DUCK WITH HARICOT BLANC, PORT DRESSING & FOIE GRAS

SERVES 4

🍷 *Leabrook Estate Pinot Gris*
(Australia)

Ingredients

2 duck breasts

Foie Gras Roulade

100g foie gras
10ml white port
10ml brandy

Port Dressing

1 tsp Dijon mustard
20ml port
150ml rapeseed oil
salt and pepper

Salad

haricot blanc
1 ltr chicken stock
2 cloves garlic
1 sprig thyme
1 large carrot
20g green beans
handful of raisins

Method

For The Roulade

De-vein and marinade the foie gras in the brandy and white port for two hours. Roll and cook in water at 55°C for three minutes.

For The Duck

Season and render the duck skin in a cold pan then sear and finish by roasting in the oven at 180°C for five minutes, then chill.

For The Dressing

Combine the Dijon mustard, rapeseed oil, port and salt and pepper and mix.

For The Salad

Soak the beans in cold water overnight, then cook in chicken stock with garlic and thyme until soft. Dice the carrots and cook in salted water until tender. Cook the green beans in salted water, then refresh in iced water and dice. Combine all the ingredients and the raisins in a bowl.

To Serve

Add the dressing to the salad and mix thoroughly, then place on the plate. Slice the duck and position on top of the salad. Place the foie gras to the side of the salad.

PAVE OF SALMON WITH PROVENCAL VEGETABLE CANNELLONI, STEAMED POTATOES & TOMATO FONDUE

SERVES 4

 Stoney Vineyards Sauvignon Blanc
(Australia)

Ingredients

4 x 140g salmon fillets
5ml rapeseed oil
knob of butter

Fondue

2kg plum tomatoes
150g caster sugar
2 garlic cloves (crushed)
1 sprig thyme
100ml white wine vinegar

Provençal Vegetables

1 small red onion
1 green pepper
1 red pepper
1 yellow pepper
1 aubergine
1 courgette

100g new potatoes
2 courgettes (slice into strips for the cannelloni)

Garnish

fresh basil
rapeseed oil

Method

For The Salmon

In a hot pan, heat 5ml of rapeseed oil. Place the salmon, skin side down, and season. Seal for one minute, turn the heat down by half and add a small amount of butter. Cook for a further two minutes until the skin is a golden colour. Turn the fish and cook for a further minute. Take off the heat and allow to rest.

For The Fondue

Blanch and refresh the tomatoes then remove the skin and seeds. Add sugar to the pan and lightly caramelise. *Deglaze* the pan with the white wine vinegar. Add the tomatoes, thyme and garlic and cook slowly on a low heat until the tomato breaks down into a purée consistency. Remove the garlic and thyme and blitz.

For The Provençal Vegetables

Dice the red onion, all the peppers, one courgette and aubergine and add to a large pan. Add a little oil and a little salt and pepper. Once softened add a couple of spoons of the tomato fondue.

For The Cannelloni

Peel strips of the courgette and *blanch* in salted water for 20 seconds and then refresh in ice cold water. On greaseproof paper, lay out five strips of courgette and place a tablespoon of the warm ratatouille on top then roll the courgettes, in a similar way to sushi, to form the cannelloni. Use straight away.

For The Potatoes

Cook the potatoes in boiling salted water for ten to 15 minutes until cooked. Serve immediately.

To Serve

Place the cannelloni on the plate with the new potatoes and salmon. Use the tomato fondue as a sauce and drizzle a little rapeseed oil over the salmon and garnish with fresh basil.

BURNT CUMIN SEED CUSTARD WITH POACHED PEARS & SEA BUCKTHORN SORBET

SERVES 4

 Coteau Du Layon
(France)

Ingredients

Cumin Seed Custard

375ml double cream
53g caster sugar
75g egg yolks
10g cumin seeds
2g fennel seeds

Poaching Syrup For Pears And Sorbet

3 ripe pears
125ml fresh sea buckthorn juice
250ml still water
100g caster sugar
30g glucose

Chocolate Crumble Mix

70g soft butter
20g cocoa powder
70g plain flour
65g caster sugar
pinch salt

Garnish

mint leaves
walnuts
sea buckthorn chocolates

Method

For The Custard

Heat and toast the cumin seeds in a dry pan until smoke starts to form. Leave to cool, then grind in a mortar. In a saucepan, combine the cream, sugar and ground cumin seeds and whole fennel seeds. Bring to a boil, then simmer for a further two minutes. Pass through a muslin cloth and add the egg yolks. Pour into four ramekins or lined moulds (can make six smaller portions) and place in a preheated oven at 95°C on a baking tray. Cook for ten to 15 minutes until completely set.

For The Syrup And Sorbet

Combine all the ingredients in a saucepan and boil. Peel pears and cut into quarters and remove the core. Place into the simmering poaching *liquor* making sure that they are completely submerged. Cover and leave on a low heat until the pears are soft. Remove pears and place in cool water to stop the cooking process. Keep the pears in half of the syrup overnight to intensify the flavour. Use the remainder of the syrup to make the sorbet by adding a little more sugar and sea buckthorn juice to taste. Churn in an ice cream maker.

For The Chocolate Crumble Mix

Mix all the ingredients together and spread onto a tray lined with greaseproof paper. Cook in a preheated oven at 180°C for ten to 15 minutes. When cool, blitz in a blender to create a fine crumble.

To Serve

Assemble as in picture and garnish with mint leaves, walnuts and speciallly selected sea buckthorn chocolates.

180
THE RESTAURANT AT THE LOVAT

Loch Ness, Fort Augustus, Inverness-shire, PH32 4DU

01456 459 250
www.thelovat.com

The Lovat is an independently owned former Victorian station hotel located in the bustling yet quaint village of Fort Augustus on the banks of Loch Ness. The 28 bedroom hotel is full of character, carefully balanced by contemporary charm. It has been nurtured by Caroline Gregory and her team, to become an award-winning, eco-conscious establishment that is attracting increasing interest as well as maintaining a loyal customer base, captivated by the hotel's naturally warm hospitality in such an iconic location.

There are two dining areas at the hotel - The Brasserie offers an à la carte menu available throughout the year. However, it is The Restaurant which highlights the true talents of head chef, Sean Kelly.

Sean is subtly ambitious and adventurous in his creativity, pushing his boundaries as well as yours. The Restaurant's concept is not to be perceived as pretentious because the experience is interesting, exciting and fun - accentuating the most important element - good food! Sean strives for perfection - from production to plate.

With five set courses, The Restaurant offers a more refined dining culinary experience that is comfortably informal yet highly professional. The emphasis is on experimental and exciting concepts that showcase Sean and his team's artistic genius!

Relish Restaurant Rewards
See page 003 for details.

Sean was pastry chef at Berties under Albert Roux
and second chef at Michelin star restaurants La Table du
Baltimore and Le Drouant. He was 'Scottish Fine Dining
Chef of the Year' in 2008, has retained two AA Rosettes
at the Lovat and now has his sight on three AA Rosettes.

Matt took third in Roux's 2012 Young Highland Chef of the
Year competition, illustrating the kitchen's determination
for success, and adding to the hotel's history of awards.

HIGHLAND BEEF, CHICKEN LIVER, BEETS FROM THE GARDEN

SERVES 4

🍷 *Delamotte Brut NV*
   (France)

Ingredients

Parfait (serves more than 4 people)

200g chicken livers
30ml port
50ml Madeira
1 garlic clove
1 shallot (chopped)
3 free range eggs
200g butter (melted)

Beetroot Jelly

100g red wine vinegar
star anise
100ml beetroot juice
50g caster sugar
3 leaves of gelatine (softened in cold water)

Tartare

240g Highland beef fillet (diced)
20g shallots (chopped)

Beetroot Meringue

60g egg white
90g icing sugar
30g beetroot powder
lemon (juice of two thirds)

To Serve

deep fried capers
lightly whipped cream, flavoured with
horseradish and lemon, season to taste

Method

For The Parfait

Boil the Madeira and port with shallots and garlic until reduced by half then cool.

Blitz the chicken livers with the eggs and the *reduction* and slowly add the melted butter. Season.

Cook in a *bain-marie* at 130°C for approximately 40 minutes or when the middle of the parfait has reached 68°C. Allow to go cold and shape into spheres then freeze.

> **Chef's Tip**
> Sit the terrine on a cloth in the *bain marie* so there isn't direct heat on the container.

For The Tartare

Mix uncooked diced beef and chopped shallots together and season. (Must use high quality ingredients for best results).

For The Beetroot Jelly

Bring all ingredients to a boil. Add the gelatine and pass through a strainer.

Dip the frozen parfait spheres into the beetroot jelly.

For Beetroot Meringue

Whisk egg whites to form soft peaks, then add half the sugar and the lemon juice. Continue to whisk until firm peaks, then add remaining sugar and beetroot powder. Whisk until firm. Spread the meringue thinly onto non-stick mats and *dehydrate* at 60° for four hours then break into pieces and store in an air tight container.

To Serve

When the parfait is defrosted it is ready to serve. Place the pickled beetroot tips on top of the parfait to resemble a baby beetroot.

Press the tartare into a ring then place the parfait, beetroot meringue and beetroot around with a few dots of horseradish cream and some crispy fried capers.

SHEPHERD'S PIE & LAMB TITBITS

SERVES 4

🍷 *Chamuyo Malbec, 2010, Mendoza Vineyards,*
(Argentina)

Ingredients

Shepherd's Pie

150g minced Scottish lamb
1 shallot (chopped)
10g carrot (diced)
100g lamb stock
10g butter
8g tomato paste
mashed potato

Titbits

200g Scottish lamb shoulder
2 garlic cloves (chopped)
3g rosemary (chopped)
3g thyme (chopped)

100g Scottish lamb sweetbreads
(soaked in water for 24hrs)
20g butter
plain flour

best end of Scottish lamb
1 garlic clove (chopped)
3g rosemary (chopped)
3g thyme (chopped)
20g butter

Pea Purée

100g frozen peas
4 mint leaves
enough water to cover

Method

For The Shepherd's Pie

Sweat the shallots in butter. Add the mince and brown, then add the tomato paste and stock and cook for ten minutes. Add the carrots and cook for a further ten minutes. Pour into a dish and pipe hot mash on top.

For The Shoulder (Titbits)

Spread garlic and herbs over the shoulder and cook in a pressure cooker for one hour. Allow to cool then shape into a cylinder. Cut into four pieces then panfry.

Chef's Tip

Roll the shoulder in clingfilm very tight to get the cylindrical shape then leave in the fridge overnight.

For The Sweetbreads

Cover with fresh water and bring to a boil. Chill, then remove the fine membrane, coat in plain flour and cook in butter until golden.

For The Best End

Season on the lamb, then panfry in butter with the garlic and herbs, keeping the lamb pink.

For The Pea Purée

Bring water to a boil with the mint leaves. Add the peas. Once cooked, strain and blitz, reserving some liquid to add to form a smooth purée.

To Serve

Spread the pea purée and arrange the shepherd's pie and lamb titbits on a hot plate. At the restaurant we serve the shepherd's pie in a potato basket.

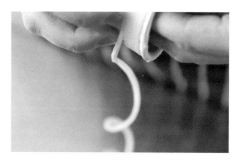

ROOT VEGETABLES

SERVES 6

 Muscat Beaumes de Venise 2009, Domaine Perrin, Rhône (France)

Ingredients

Carrot Mousse

200g white chocolate
100g carrot purée (100g carrot chopped into
small pieces, carrot juice to cover)
2 free range eggs (separated)
200g whipped cream
(no sugar used as white chocolate is quite sweet)

Chocolate And Beetroot Mousse

200g dark chocolate
100g beetroot purée (100g whole beetroot,
water to cover)
2 eggs (separated)
200g whipped cream
40g caster sugar

Parsnip And Vanilla Sponge Cake

150g parsnip purée (150g parsnips chopped into
small pieces, milk to cover)
100g caster sugar
1 free range egg
90g plain flour
8g baking powder
1 vanilla pod

Carrot Sorbet

600g carrot juice
180g caster sugar
30g glucose syrup
1 lemon (juice of)
1 leaf gelatine (softened in cold water)

Tubes

100g carrot purée
100g beetroot purée
60g glucose (30g for each purée)

Method

For The Parsnip And Vanilla Sponge Cake

Whisk the egg with the sugar until doubled in size. Fold in the flour and baking powder. Scrape seeds from the vanilla pod into the parsnip purée then fold this into the mix. Pour into a square cake tin (large enough to take 500g) and cook at 160°C for approximately 35 minutes.

For The Purées

Cook the vegetable in the liquid until soft. Strain, reserving the liquid. Blitz the vegetable, adding reserved liquid to obtain a smooth purée (should be quite a dry consistency).

For The Carrot Sorbet

Reduce carrot juice until you have 500g. Add sugar, syrup and lemon juice and stir until dissolved. Squeeze gelatine, then add to the liquid. Allow to go cold then churn in an ice cream machine.

For The Mousses

Melt the chocolate in a bowl over a pan of hot water. Whisk egg whites and sugar together. When the chocolate has melted, add the egg yolks and purée. Fold in the egg whites and cream. Pour mixture into six small 75ml ramekins and allow to set.

> **Chef's Tip**
>
> Make sure that the eggs are at room temperature so that the chocolate doesn't set straight away.

For The Tubes

Mix 30g of glucose into 100g of each purée. Spread each mixture thinly into a square shape. Cook at 130°C for 30 minutes.
Take out of the oven, quickly remove the squares and wrap the heated purée around a tube to get the shape.

To Serve

Fill the tubes with the mousse. Arrange the different desserts on a cold plate.

190
RESTAURANT MARK GREENAWAY

69 North Castle Street, Edinburgh EH2 3LJ

0131 226 1155
www.restaurantmarkgreenaway.com

Mark Greenaway received nationwide acclaim following the opening of his eponymous restaurant in Edinburgh in February 2011. The following January Mark was the only Scottish chef to be newly awarded three AA Rosettes for outstanding cuisine.

With a passion for Scottish ingredients, Mark and his small team use only the very best local, seasonal produce, transforming them into modern versions of traditional classics such as cullen skink and Eton mess. The menus are always intriguing with a presentation that is pleasing to both eye and palate. Mark's signature style is desserts; a visit to Restaurant Mark Greenaway is an invitation to indulge in dessert. The spectacular eight course 'Tour Menu' is a great way to sample Mark's inventive cooking style.

The Wine Vault

Renowned for its vibrant mix of diners and exciting menus, Restaurant Mark Greenaway brings understated glamour to Edinburgh's dining scene and in January 2013 the restaurant moved to a new, more central location in Edinburgh's New Town.

The beautiful Georgian building houses an old bank vault which has been converted into a specially-designed wine room, where sommelier Loic Druyver invites diners to sample wine before ordering. A private dining room seating up to 12 people is also available.

The 60-seater restaurant is open Tuesday to Saturday for lunch and dinner.

Renowned for its vibrant mix of diners and exciting menus, Restaurant Mark Greenaway brings understated glamour to Edinburgh's dining scene.

MODERN CULLEN SKINK

SERVES 4

 Albariño Rias Baixas
(Spain)

Ingredients

2 ltr full fat milk
4 fillets smoked haddock (de-boned)
2 leeks
20 pearl onions
2 large Maris piper potatoes (peeled)
1 tsp olive oil

Garnish

dill
chives
2 dtsp caviar (optional)

Method

Cut four large diamond shapes from the haddock fillets and set aside. Chop remaining haddock into small pieces.

Cut potatoes into large rectangles (big enough to sit the diamond of haddock on). Cut the rest of the potatoes into small dice.

Slice the white of the leek into 20 rounds and set aside. Dice the remainder of the leek and set aside.

Blanch the peeled pearl onions in a little salted water until just cooked (keep warm).

Blanch the large rectangle of potato in boiling salted water until just cooked (keep warm).

Put the milk, diced leeks, haddock and small diced potatoes in a heavy based pan and simmer for about ten minutes. Once tender and cooked, blend until smooth (keep warm).

Meanwhile, place a teaspoon of olive oil in a non-stick pan and cook haddock diamonds on nicest looking side first until cooked halfway through. Add leek rounds to pan and cook until the fish is completely cooked and leeks have nicely coloured.

Check the milk mixture for seasoning and season to taste.

To Serve

Assemble and garnish on deep plates as pictured and serve the soup mixture separately and let your guests pour it themselves.

Chef's Tip

Serve with a small quenelle of caviar on top of the haddock to add a little something special.

PAN SEARED HAKE FILLET, LOBSTER TORTELLINI, BUTTERNUT SQUASH, FENNEL & DILL PUREE, RADISH, SAFFRON BROTH

SERVES 4

 Viognier, Marlborough
(New Zealand)

Ingredients

Fish
4 x 40g piece hake (skin on, bones removed)
25g butter (per piece of hake)
rapeseed oil
squeeze of lemon
sea salt

Pasta Dough
11 egg yolks
500g pasta flour
3 whole eggs
10ml olive oil

Paste Filling
1 lobster
1 whole egg
150ml double cream
salt (to taste)
dill

Fennel And Dill Purée
1 head fennel
60g butter
2 shallots
1/2 bunch dill
1 small clove garlic
100ml fish stock
100ml milk
100ml double cream

Broth
1/2 ltr fish stock
pinch saffron
spoonful diced fennel

Vegetable
1/2 butternut squash

Garnish
baby basil
sliced radish

Method

For The Pasta Dough
Rub egg yolks through flour. Add olive oil. Add whole eggs one by one until dough comes to the right consistency. Rest for ten minutes. Roll out on a lightly-floured surface and pass through a pasta machine until the second last setting. Cut 4" circles with pastry cutter.

For The Paste Filling
Kill the lobster by thrusting a knife through its brain. Cut lobster in half. In a pan, roast half the lobster and one claw in a medium hot (185°C) oven for six minutes. Once cooked, remove the meat and dice. Pick the raw meat from the rest of the lobster including the claw and blend with an egg in a food processor. In a bowl, add half the cream to the blended raw lobster mix. Then add the cooked lobster meat and the rest of the cream and chopped dill. Chill for 20 minutes.

To Make And Cook The Tortellini
Place a spoonful of the lobster mix in the centre of each pasta round. Fold in half to form a semi-circle and seal edges with fingers. Pull both ends together to form a tortellini shape. Cook in boiling, salted water for three minutes.

For The Fennel And Dill Purée
Finely slice fennel, garlic and shallots (reserve a little fennel for the broth). Melt butter and cook out vegetables until slightly soft. Pour over milk and cream. Simmer for 15 minutes. Add dill and blend until smooth and at the correct consistency. Pass through a fine sieve and keep warm until ready to plate up.

For The Broth
Add all ingredients to a pan and warm. Reduce by half.

For The Butternut Squash
Dice and *blanch* butternut squash. Keep warm until needed.

For The Fish
Heat the rapeseed oil in a non-stick pan. Place the hake in the heat, skin side down. Cook for three or four minutes until lightly coloured. Place the pan in a hot oven for two to three minutes, depending on thickness of fish. Finish with a knob of butter, a squeeze of lemon juice and a sprinkling of sea salt.

Chef's Tip
Ask your fishmonger to de-bone and fillet the fish for you. After all, that's what they're there for!

To Serve
Serve as pictured. In the restaurant we serve this dish with mashed purple potato quenelles.

Eton Mess

SERVES 4

 *Liqueur Muscat, Clare Valley
(Australia)*

Ingredients

Strawberry Custard Jelly

6 egg yolks
120g caster sugar
500ml homemade strawberry coulis (no sugar)
6 sheets gelatine (soaked in cold water)

Meringue

150g egg whites (room temperature)
280g caster sugar

Strawberry Fluid Gel

600ml fresh strawberry juice
150g caster sugar
6g gellan gum

Strawberry Leather

100g strawberry purée
80g icing sugar
1/2 tsp crispfilm

Marshmallows

11 leaves gelatine
245g cold water
450g granulated sugar
375g glucose
125g water
1/2 tsp salt
3 vanilla pods
caster sugar (for dredging)

Crème Chantilly

400ml double cream
seeds from 1 vanilla pod
60g icing sugar

Extras

20 strawberries
frozen raspberry cells (freeze raspberries then
break up, store in freezer until ready to use)
1 packet micro red basil

Chef's Tip

Buy the freshest local strawberries you can lay your
hands on and always use at room temperature for
maximum flavour.

Method

For The Strawberry Custard Jelly

Put everything in a thermomix (or blender) and blend on number
six until 80°C is reached. Add gelatine and continue to blend for a
further three minutes. Pass through a fine strainer onto a
clingfilmed tray. Pull clingfilm back until 1cm thickness is achieved.
Set in fridge for four hours and then cut into 1cm cubes.
Return to the fridge until ready to use.

For The Meringue

Whip meringue on a medium speed until soft peaks are achieved.
Slowly add the sugar in a steady stream until all the sugar is
incorporated and a stiff peak is achieved. Spread thinly on
silicone paper and dry out in an oven with the pilot on overnight
or, alternatively, in a hot plate set at the lowest setting. Once dry,
break into shards and store in an airtight container.

For The Strawberry Fluid Gel

Rub gellan through sugar. Mix strawberry juice with sugar.
Bring to a boil slowly and pass through *chinois*. Chill in a
suitable container for approximately 30 minutes. Once set,
blend on medium speed for approximately ten minutes until
smooth. Pass through fine *chinois*. Put mixture in a squeezy
bottle until required.

For The Strawberry Leather

Blend all ingredients and pass through a fine *chinois* onto a
silicon mat. Dry out under hot lights or in a *dehydrator*. Cut into
triangles whilst still warm and store in between greaseproof
paper in an airtight container.

For The Marshmallows

Soak gelatine in 245g cold water until soft. Pour into mixing
bowl and whisk. Combine sugar, glucose and 125g water and
boil rapidly for one and a half minutes. Pour boiling syrup into
gelatine, then mix and whisk for exactly 12 minutes. Scrape into
a tray lined with clingfilm (oil tray before putting in clingfilm)
and press fresh clingfilm into it to flatten it out. Leave to set in
fridge for four hours.

To Build The Dish

Gather together all your prepared items and four cold plates.
Wash and cut half of the total strawberries in half leaving the
other half as they are. Scatter the strawberries evenly between
all the plates.

Place four cubes of the custard jelly onto each plate and dot the
fluid gel around the jelly and strawberries. Cut marshmallow
into 1cm by 3cm pieces and dredge in caster sugar. Using a
blowtorch, lightly toast the top of each marshmallow. Quenelle
three teaspoons of crème Chantilly onto each plate. Scatter the
meringue and frozen raspberry cells around the plate. Top off
with baby basil and strawberry leather.

200
ROCCA BAR & GRILL

The Links, St Andrews, Fife, KY16 9JQ

01334 472 549
www.roccagrill.com

Rocca Bar And Grill came to life in February 2010 under the ownership of Adrian and Susan Pieraccini and since then, it has gone from strength to strength. Adrian and Susan are no strangers to the restaurant trade. With numerous successes under their belts, their winning formula has now been applied to Rocca.

Rocca's beautiful, lush décor is testament to Susan's artistic finesse whilst Adrian's Italian flair bursts out of the kitchen and onto the plate. Rocca's food and ideals are straight forward - keep it simple and be the best - a vision shared by the whole team.

Our close team of passionate and skilled chefs has lifted Rocca to be one of the finest dining experiences on the beautiful east coast of Fife in Scotland. But it's not just our exceptional award-winning food that makes Rocca one of the best - the front of house is led by our manageress Sue McKay and her talented team of bubbly and knowledgeable staff. Sue's energetic approach to service is palpable and shines through the team, who are proud of the food they serve and passionate about Rocca's ideals.

We are set a golf ball's throw away from the world famous Old Course and our incredible view overlooks the 18th green, out over to the champagne beach of the West Sands - an exquisite vista unique to the Rocca Bar And Grill.

Our formula works. Rocca was awarded its third AA Rosette award in early 2012 for exceptional food, service and ambience - our core values.

Relish Restaurant Rewards
See page 003 for details.

In its first year of opening Rocca was awarded 'Rising Star' by the Scottish hotel awards and 'Best New Business of the Year' from SLTN. Since then Rocca has gone from strength to strength and has now been awarded with its third AA Rosette for outstanding food, service and ambience. A culmination of teamwork and dedication has led us to this prestigious award - something we are very proud of.

ROASTED HAND-DIVED SCALLOPS, BUTTERNUT SQUASH GNOCCHI, CRISPY SWEETBREAD, PANCETTA & CHESTNUTS

SERVES 4

*Pomino Bianco, Marchesi di Frescobaldi 2010
(Italy)*

Ingredients

12 medium hand-dived scallops
(cleaned and roe removed)
1 lemon (juice of)
200g peeled lamb sweetbreads (soaked in milk for
12 hours)
flour, butter and thyme (to coat)

Butternut Squash Gnocchi

large pinch salt
1 sprig thyme
bulb garlic (cut in half)
200g puréed butternut squash (roasted with the
salt, thyme and garlic the puréed and hung in
muslin for 12 hours)
500g (2 large potatoes) hot dry mash potato.
40g parmesan (grated)
1 egg
1 egg yolk
130g pasta flour
salt, pepper and nutmeg

Chestnut Purée

350g pack cooked chestnuts
100ml chicken stock
100ml double cream

Garnish

100g smoked pancetta (frozen and sliced thinly)

Method

For The Butternut Squash (Prepare the day before)

De-seed the butternut squash and split in half, the day before. Roast the butternut in the oven with salt, thyme and garlic, until tender. Remove flesh and pass through a sieve. Hang in a muslin overnight in the fridge to allow the moisture to drip out.

For The Gnocchi

Peel two large potatoes and cook in seasoned water, until tender. Drain then place back in a pan and dry out. Pass through a sieve and add the butternut squash, parmesan and seasoning. Mix well then add eggs and pasta flour. Place mixture in a piping bag and pipe into clingfilm (a diameter of 2.5cm). Roll and tie the end. Repeat until mixture is finished. Cook in lightly simmering water for ten minutes.

Remove from the water and allow to cool, then place in the refrigerator.

For The Chestnut Purée

Reserve six whole chestnuts and spilt in two. Boil the chicken stock and double cream. Add the remaining chestnuts and cook for two minutes. Strain the liquid off and keep aside. Place the chestnuts in a food processor and purée. Add liquid until you get a smooth purée, season and strain through a sieve.

For The Pancetta

Cook in the oven between greaseproof paper at 160°C for ten to 12 minutes, or until golden brown and crisp. Remove onto a cloth, set aside.

To Serve

Cut gnocchi into 1cm discs and panfry on both side until golden brown. Add butter, foam then add the six halved chestnuts. Warm the chestnut purée.

Cook scallops until golden then turn over and add butter and lemon juice. Coat the sweetbreads in seasoned flour and shallow fry until golden and crispy on both sides. Add butter and thyme. Remove all ingredients on to a draining cloth and plate. Finish with pancetta.

ROASTED VENISON LOIN FROM FORFAR & SMOKED BEETROOT CONSOMME, CELERIAC & THYME DUMPLING, ROASTED SALSIFY

SERVES 4

Syrah Fuedo Butera, 2009
(Italy)

Ingredients

400g trimmed venison loin
(cut into 100g portions)
butter, thyme, 1 garlic clove

Smoked Beetroot Consommé

2kg venison bones
200g oak wood chips
3 carrots (peeled and diced)
2 sticks celery (diced)
1 large red beetroot (diced)
200g button mushroom (sliced)
6 shallots (sliced)
2 cloves garlic, 2 sprigs thyme
1 star anise, 1 bay leaf, 6 black peppercorns
100ml Madeira, 100ml port
2 ltr brown chicken stock
185g venison trim
100g egg whites
smoked Maldon salt

Celeriac And Thyme Dumpling

350g celeriac (cooked and peeled - hang in muslin overnight)
350g (2 medium potatoes) hot, dry mash potato
40g finely grated parmesan
1 egg, 1 egg yolk
130g 00 pasta flour
1 tsp picked chopped thyme
knob of butter

Garnish

2 sticks salsify
1 lemon (juice of)
1 large beetroot
1 sprig thyme, 2 cloves garlic
6 pickling/baby onions
6 pieces chervil (optional)
200g baby spinach (picked and washed)
100g pied de mouton
Maldon sea salt
butter (for panfrying)

Method

For The Venison Loin

Cook the venison loin at 56°C in a water bath for 40 minutes. Or you can cook the venison in the oven until medium rare.

For The Consommé

Add the chopped venison bones onto the second level of a steamer pot, above smoking woodchips. Seal lid and smoke the bones for 30 minutes.

Fry the smoked venison bones until a light golden colour. Add two carrots, celery, two cloves garlic and three quarters of the beetroot. Season and roast for five to six minutes. Add half the mushrooms and all the shallots. Cook for a further two minutes. Add one sprig of thyme, bay leaf, peppercorns and star anise. Cook for two minutes, then add Madeira and port and reduce by two thirds.

Add the chicken stock, bring to a simmer and cook for one and a half hours. Strain through a fine sieve and reduce down to one litre. Once reduced, check seasoning and cool to blood temperature (37°C).

Blitz together venison trimmings, egg whites, the remaining carrot, sprig of thyme, quarter of the beetroot and remaining mushrooms. Whisk into the venison stock over a medium heat until the first bubble rises. Remove, whisk and reduce the heat making a small well in the middle - be careful not to break the raft floating on top. Simmer for a further ten minutes then strain through a muslin. Set aside.

For The Celeriac And Thyme Dumpling (Prepare the day before)

Mix together the cooked, dried out potatoes, cooked celeriac, parmesan, thyme and seasoning. Once mixed, add the egg, egg yolk and flour and mix well. Heat in boiling water for two minutes then toss in butter and thyme (optional) just before serving.

For The Garnish

Roast the beetroot in tinfoil with rock salt, thyme and garlic at 140°C for one hour or until tender. Cut into 1cm cubes. Peel one salsify then cut into thin strips and deep fry at 140°C until a light golden brown. Season. Peel the other salsify then cook in lemon seasoned water until just tender. Cut into 7cm pieces and split in half.

To Serve

Take the venison out of water bath, season and pan roast on all sides. Add butter, thyme and garlic clove. Remove from pan and rest. In a separate pan, roast the salsify, baby onions and beetroot in foaming butter. Sauté the spinach, warm the other ingredients and assemble as in picture.

CRUNCHY PASSION FRUIT CREAM, COCONUT SORBET, TEXTURES & FLAVOURS OF PISTACHIO, MANGO, SALT & WHITE CHOCOLATE

SERVES 4

 Recioto di Soave 'Rocca Sveve'
(Italy)

Ingredients

Passion Fruit Cream
3 eggs, 6 egg yolks
250g caster sugar, 300g double cream
10 passion fruit (juiced)

Pistachio And Polenta Cake
70g soft unsalted butter
75g caster sugar
5g pistachio compound, 60g whole egg
45g ground almonds
20g ground peeled pistachio
$1/2$ tsp baking powder
42g fine polenta, 2 tbsp plain flour, pinch salt

White Chocolate Crisp
42g glucose, 42g Isomalt, 82g fondant
37g white chocolate

Mango Purée
1 ripe mango
25g caster sugar, 0.5g agar agar

Salted Crumble
100g plain flour, 50g caster sugar
50g hard, unsalted butter
2g Maldon sea salt
2g salt
(crumb ingredients together and bake on metal tray at
160°C until golden brown)

Coconut Sorbet
450g coconut cream
50g Malibu
1 lime (juice of), 75g caster sugar
(boil sugar and coconut cream, add lime juice and
Malibu then cool - churn in a ice cream machine)

Garnish
caramelised pistachios

Method

For The Passion Fruit Cream
Reduce passion fruit juice to 100ml. Add cream and bring to a boil. Whisk eggs, yolk and sugar together. Pour cream onto egg mixture and whisk. Lightly grease and line a metal tray with a double sheet of clingfilm, 10cm by 15cm by 2.5cm.

Skim off foam from the passion fruit mixture and pour into the lined tray and place in a preheated oven at 90°C, half fan.
Cook for about 30 minutes or until set. Set aside in the fridge for a minimum of two hours.

For The Pistachio And Polenta Cake
Beat the soft butter, pistachio compound and caster sugar together until white and aerated. Add egg then beat. Fold in all dry ingredients and mix.

Pour the mixture into a greased and lined bread loaf tin, 27cm by 8cm. Bake at 140°C covered for 20 minutes. Remove cover and cook for a further ten minutes until light golden brown. Remove from tin, cool on wire rack and refrigerate.

For The Mango Purée
Peel mango and remove flesh from stone. Blitz flesh and sugar until smooth and pass through a fine sieve. Weigh 100g of the mango purée and pour into a small pan then add agar agar. Whisk and leave to stand for ten minutes. Bring gently to a boil, whisking as you do so. Simmer for one minute. Remove from the heat and cool. Once set, blitz until a smooth and glossy purée is formed, then pass again and set aside.

For The White Chocolate Crisp
Melt glucose, Isomalt and fondant in a pan, cook to 158°C. Cool to 153°C and add white chocolate. Mix well and pour on to a silicon mat. Once hard, blitz to a powder. Sieve a thin layer over a silicon mat and cook at 150°C until melted. Cool and set aside.

To Serve
Cut passion fruit cream into 14cm by 2cm pieces, cover with a line layer of caster sugar and blow torch until caramelised. Spoon the crumble around, dot with purée and caramelised pistachio. Cut pistachio cake into 2cm squared pieces, warm the pistachio cake and arrange three pieces on the plate. Decorate with the crisp and finish with homemade coconut sorbet (see ingredients for instruction) or alternatively buy it ready-made.

210
THE SEAFOOD RESTAURANT

Bruce Embankment, St Andrews, Fife, KY16 9AB

01334 479 475
www.theseafoodrestaurant.com

The Seafood Restaurant, in St Andrews, has changed the food scene in the area since its opening in August 2003. The restaurant offers modern, contemporary dining in an outstanding location, with magnificent views over West Sands, the Old Course golf links beyond, and the North Sea. With windows from floor to ceiling, the restaurant feels light and airy and is a perfect backdrop for the freshest of seafood, sourced from the shores below the restaurant and around Scotland.

With a passion for sustainability, locally reared meat and game offer superb choices to try out the recognised wine list. Head chef Colin Fleming and his team cooks in the open kitchen, providing an insight into the clean, fresh flavours that speak for themselves.

St Andrews is one of Scotland's most popular destinations and is a 'must' for all golf fans and tourists. The Seafood Restaurant is one of St Andrews' most popular places to dine. Watching the sun set over the Old Course while eating from Chef Fleming's menus is the highlight of many visitor's stay.

The Seafood Restaurant has won such accolades as AA Scottish Restaurant of the Year, Good Food Guide Newcomer of the Year and the AA Wine List of the Year.

Relish Restaurant Rewards
See page 003 for details.

We specialise in the best of Scottish seafood, with produce ranging from West Coast mussels, scallops and oysters to the best St Andrew's Bay lobsters, Pittenweem crab and North Sea fish landed at Aberdeen fish market. Carnivores and vegetarians are well catered for with locally reared meat and game, and many fruit and vegetables grown in the regions of Fife and Tayside.

HAND-DIVED SCALLOPS, SWEET & SOUR CABBAGE, BROWN SHRIMP, CHESTNUT

SERVES 4

🍷 *Savennières, Clos du Papillon, Domaine des Baumard 2006, Loire (France)*

Ingredients

12 hand-dived scallops

Brown Shrimp Cream

500ml fish stock
200ml double cream
125ml white wine
5g brown shrimps
1 banana shallot (finely sliced)
1 garlic clove (finely sliced)
1 bunch of chopped chervil (keep stalks)
1 tsp wholegrain mustard
$^1/_2$ tsp honey
lemon juice (squeeze of)

Chestnut Purée

200ml whole milk
20ml water
200g chestnuts (finely chopped)
1 roasted chestnut (set aside for shaving)
knob of butter

White Cabbage

500g white cabbage (finely sliced)
5g pinenuts (toasted)
5g golden raisins (soaked in rum)
1 tbsp sherry vinegar

Method

For The Cream

Sweat the shallot and garlic until soft, add white wine. Reduce down, add fish stock and reduce by one third. Add the cream and boil for five minutes, then remove from heat. Add the chervil stalks. Season to taste and set aside.

For The Chestnut Purée

Bring the milk and water to a boil, add chestnuts and cook for five minutes. Blitz to make a purée then gradually add the butter.

For The Cabbage

Blanch the cabbage in boiling water for five minutes or until tender. Add pinenuts, raisins and sherry vinegar. Season.

For The Scallops

Heat a non-stick frying pan with a dash of cooking oil. Add scallops for two minutes, remove from pan and season. Meanwhile, return to cream and gently warm through. Finish cream with honey, mustard, lemon juice, shrimps and chervil leaves.

To Serve

Assemble the dish and shave chestnut over plate.

Chef's Tip

I like to use micro celery leaves for garnishing.

TURBOT, HERB CRUST, BABY ARTICHOKES, SMOKED BACON, CRAB BEIGNETS

SERVES 4

🍷 *Mercurey 'Les Montots', Domaine A&P de Villaine 2009, Burgundy (France)*

Ingredients

4 turbot portions
12 smoked pancetta buttons
5g trompette de la mort mushrooms
knob of butter

Herb Crust

150g brioche
70g butter (melted)
20g Gruyère cheese (finely grated)
70g flat leaf parsley
20g chervil, 1 tsp picked thyme

Salsa Verde

1/2 bunch flat leaf parsley
10g basil, 10g mint
4 anchovies
50ml olive oil
1 tbsp Dijon mustard

Jerusalem Artichoke Purée

500g Jerusalem artichokes
200ml double cream
100ml water, knob of butter

Crab Beignets

200g picked white crab meat
75g dry mash potato
75g dried breadcrumbs
1 bunch flat leaf parsley (chopped)
2 tbsp artichoke purée
1 lemon (juice)

Potato Crisps

200g dry mash potato
1 egg white, knob of butter
5g chives (finely chopped)

Baby Artichokes

8 baby artichokes
1 sprig thyme, 1 lemon (juice)

Garnish

sea purslane

Method

For The Herb Crust

Blitz all ingredients in a blender to make a paste and season well with salt. Roll out on clingfilm to a thickness of half a centimetre and freeze.

For The Salsa Verde

Blitz all ingredients to make a purée, add seasoning and set aside.

For The Jerusalem Artichoke Purée

Peel and slice artichokes and sweat in butter until soft. Add water and reduce, then add cream and reduce. Remove from heat and season with salt. Blitz in a blender and pass through a fine sieve. Set aside.

For The Crab Beignets

Combine all ingredients and mix thoroughly. Shape into small balls and *pané* in parsley breadcrumbs. Refrigerate for two to three hours until firm to touch.

For The Potato Crisps

Place dry mash into a mixing bowl with egg white, chives and butter. Mix until smooth. Roll out to 2 to 3mm thickness and use templates as stencils to mould mixture into a flat circle. Shallow fry for 30 seconds and set aside.

For The Baby Artichokes

Peel artichokes and place them whole into a pan with the water, lemon juice and thyme. Bring to a boil and cook artichokes until tender.

To Serve

Remove the herb crust from freezer and cut to size of fillets. Heat a frying pan with cooking oil and sear the turbot on both sides for three minutes. Remove from heat and season. Place herb crust over fillets and grill with crust side facing upwards until crust has melted. Fry pancetta until golden brown and sweat trompettes in butter for one minute. Deep fry the crab beignets for two minutes and warm the purée. Assemble the dish, being careful with the potato crisps. I like to scatter the trompettes and add sea purslane, a delicious salty sea herb.

RHUBARB JELLY, POACHED RHUBARB, MILK MOUSSE, STRAWBERRY SORBET

SERVES 4

 Beerenauslese, Terrassen, Domäne Wachau 2011 (Austria)

Ingredients

Rhubarb Jelly
350g rhubarb (sliced)
100g caster sugar
200ml water
1 orange (juice)
4 gelatine leaves

Rhubarb Purée
200g rhubarb
20g caster sugar, 30ml water

Isomalt Tuile
150ml rhubarb purée
10ml liquid glucose
15g isomalt (available in specialist food shops)
1g xanthan gum (available in specialist food shops)

Milk Mousse
345ml whole milk
155ml double cream
55g caster sugar
1$\frac{1}{2}$ gelatine leaves

Poached Rhubarb
100g rhubarb (peeled and equally diced)
20g caster sugar
100ml water
50ml grenadine

Strawberry Purée
300g strawberries (halved)
20g caster sugar, 30ml water

Strawberry Sorbet
250g strawberry purée
200ml *stock syrup* (bring 200ml water and 50g caster sugar to a boil until all the sugar has dissolved. It can go into the ice cream mixer hot or cold)

Garnish
baby mint
dried rhubarb

Method

For The Rhubarb Jelly
Place all ingredients in a large pan and bring to a boil. Leave on heat until all the sugar has dissolved. Allow to cool for five minutes before whisking in soaked gelatine. Reserve some liquid and set in a deep tray lined with clingfilm. Chill until firm.

For The Rhubarb Purée
Sweat down the rhubarb on a medium heat until soft then add the sugar and water, keep on a low heat until the sugar has dissolved. Then blend in a food processor until smooth and chill until cold (approximately one to two hours). Note: add more or less sugar depending on tartness of rhubarb.

For The Isomalt Tuile
Place all ingredients in a bowl over a pan of boiling water. Whisk until thickened and quickly mould into a template. Cook at 120°C for 35 to 40 minutes and mould to acquired shape, while hot.

For The Milk Mousse
Simmer cream, milk and sugar for three minutes until the sugar has dissolved. Allow to cool slightly before whisking in gelatine. Place in cream whipper with two gas chargers or whip the cream. Chill for three to four hours.

For The Strawberry Purée
Sweat down the strawberries on a medium heat until soft then add the sugar and water and keep on a low heat until the sugar has dissolved. Then blend in a food processor until smooth and chill until cold (approximately one to two hours). Note: add more or less sugar depending on tartness of the strawberries.

For The Strawberry Sorbet
Place ingredients into an ice cream mixer and churn until firm.

For The Poached Rhubarb
Bring sugar, water and grenadine to a boil. Add rhubarb and simmer for five minutes until softened.

To Serve
Dice jelly to the same size as the cubes of rhubarb. Place the jelly and rhubarb into a 7cm moulding ring and cover with a quenelle of sorbet. Pipe over mousse, adding tuile on top. Decorate with rhubarb juice and garnish with baby mint and dried rhubarb.

220
THE SHIP ON THE SHORE
SEAFOOD RESTAURANT & CHAMPAGNE BAR

24-26 Shore, Edinburgh, EH6 6QN

0131 555 0409
www.theshiponthshore.co.uk

With Murray and Tracey Georgeson at the helm, The Ship on the Shore has been impressing seafood lovers for the past six years. Firmly established as a gourmet destination, the restaurant combines a wide variety of fresh Scottish seafood with Champagne and wines. In atmospheric surroundings in the heart of the Shore, the restaurant is fronted with a dining terrace that faces on to the water of Leith.

Murray and Tracey say "living in Scotland we have the opportunity to explore and enjoy the freshest and most extraordinary fish and seafood. We love the food in nature's larder served with Champagne and fine wines and we wanted to share what we enjoy with our fellow travellers. Our approach is simple really; we offer the finest ingredients, passionately prepared and expertly presented. At The Ship on the Shore we offer informal, understated excellence".

Head chef Willie Lonnie leads the excellent kitchen team. Willie has worked as a chef for 20 years and has never lost his passion for his job. He began his career in the kitchen of a busy city hotel where he learned the basics of his trade. His first love is, of course seafood, especially Scottish.

Willie and his team strive to improve the food at every opportunity and will always continue to do so. Willie believes that progress is essential and approaches the menu paying attention to sustainability and seasonality in a manner that reflects the best of Scottish seafood. After working in many different styles of places and environments, Willie is confident that he is achieving this goal at The Ship on the Shore.

SEAFOOD BAR

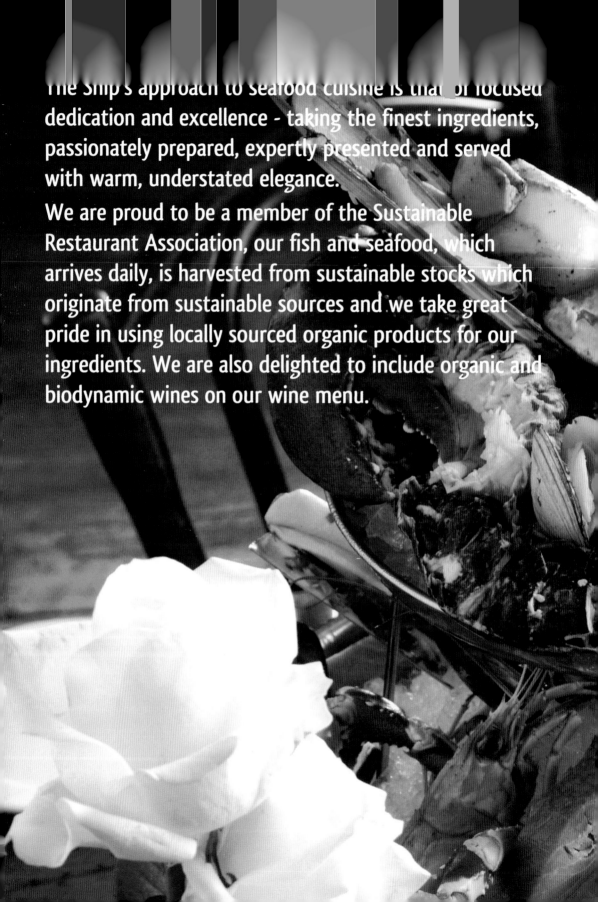

The Ship's approach to seafood cuisine is that of focused dedication and excellence - taking the finest ingredients, passionately prepared, expertly presented and served with warm, understated elegance.

We are proud to be a member of the Sustainable Restaurant Association, our fish and seafood, which arrives daily, is harvested from sustainable stocks which originate from sustainable sources and we take great pride in using locally sourced organic products for our ingredients. We are also delighted to include organic and biodynamic wines on our wine menu.

ROAST LANGOUSTINE BISQUE WITH BEETROOT ROUILLE & BASIL OIL

SERVES 4

*Muscadet de Sevre et Maine sur Lie, Ch.Haute,
Cariziere (France)
Classic, refreshing Muscadet with extra lift from
'sur lie' ageing. A truly great wine with seafood.*

Ingredients

Bisque

4 garlic cloves
1 large white onion
2 carrots
2 sticks celery
1 leek
20ml white wine
2 star anise
10g fennel seed
18 langoustines
2 tbsp tomato paste
150g butter
2 bay leaves
200ml double cream
1 ltr water

Rouille

2 beetroot
60ml olive oil
10g basil
30g white bread
1 clove garlic
1/2 lemon (juice of)
salt and pepper

Method

For The Bisque

Roast langoustines with half the butter at 180°C for five minutes. Remove tail meat and put aside. Fine dice onions, celery, carrots and leeks and gently sweat until soft. Add star anise, fennel seeds, garlic, langoustine claws and shells, add white wine and brandy and reduce. Then add tomato purée and bay leaves then water and reduce for one hour. Blend then pass through fine a sieve. To finish add cream and seasoning.

> **Chef's Tip**
> When langoustines are roasted and tails removed, cut down the back of the tail and remove waste track.

For The Rouille

Boil beetroot for 45 minutes, cool, then peel. Add the beetroot and olive oil into a blender and mix. Now add basil, garlic and finally white bread - no crusts. Season to taste.

To Serve

Place one quarter of bisque into bowl, garnish with peeled de-veined langoustines tails and one teaspoon of rouille.

CRISPY MONKFISH CHEEKS WITH ROAST PORK BELLY, SWEET POTATO FONDANT & RED PEPPER COULIS & BUTTERED SAMPHIRE GRASS

SERVES 4

🍷 *Pinot Gris Home Block Vineyard, Mudhouse, Waipara (New Zealand)*
This wine exhibits delicate aromas of pear, honeysuckle and gingerbread, leading to lively peach and pear flavours with a rich spicy finish.

Ingredients

Monkfish Cheeks
400g monkfish cheeks
1 packet Panko breadcrumbs
1 egg
100ml milk
100g plain flour

Pork Belly
200g pork belly
3 tbsp olive oil
3 sprigs thyme
2 cloves garlic
salt and pepper

Sweet Potato Fondant
4 large sweet potatoes
150g unsalted butter
2 garlic cloves
2 sprigs thyme
100ml water

Red Pepper Coulis
2 large red peppers (prepared and chopped)
2 onions (chopped)
3 cloves garlic (chopped)
1 stick celery (chopped)
2 tbsp red wine vinegar
20g brown sugar
100ml water
salt and pepper to taste

Buttered Samphire Grass
150g samphire grass
20g butter
1/2 lemon

Method

For The Monkfish Cheeks
In three separate bowls place the flour, beaten egg and milk and Panko breadcrumbs. Place monkfish cheeks in flour then the egg and milk and finally in breadcrumbs, then repeat the process.

For The Pork Belly
Take pork belly and rub chopped thyme, garlic, olive oil, salt and pepper. Place in a deep roasting tray, cover with foil and allow to roast at 150°C for two hours.

> **Chef's Tip**
> When pork belly is cooked, place between two sheets of greaseproof paper and press using two trays with a weight on a top.

For The Fondants
Using a 3cm cutter shape potatoes then gently fry in *clarified butter* until golden on top. Add whole peeled garlic cloves, 100ml water, salt and pepper and a sprig of thyme then cook for 20 minutes in the oven at 170°C.

For The Red Pepper Coulis
Sweat off onions, leeks, celery and garlic without colouring, then add peppers and even out until soft. Boil the vinegar and sugar until it reduces by half. Next, add water and bring to a boil and season with salt and pepper to taste. Simmer for 15 to 20 minutes, blend then sieve to remove any skins.

For The Buttered Samphire
Wash samphire, melt butter and add samphire grass, sauté for two minutes. Season with salt and pepper and add juice of half a lemon.

To Serve
Panfry monkfish cheeks for two minutes on each side then dry on kitchen paper. Cut pork belly into four portions. Sauté the samphire grass with 30g butter. Place three fondants on each plate. Arrange the pork belly then add dried monkfish cheeks, buttered samphire grass and red pepper coulis.

PAIN AU CHOCOLAT & CROISSANT BREAD & BUTTER PUDDING WITH VANILLA POD ICE CREAM, RHUBARB & APPLE COMPOTE

SERVES 4

Monbazillac, Domaine de l'Ancienne Cure, South West (France)
Honey and marzipan dominate the palate with confied orange peel and spices characters.

Ingredients

Bread And Butter Pudding

6 croissants
6 pain au chocolat
100ml double cream
120g caster sugar
6 eggs
100g chocolate chips
1 vanilla pod

Vanilla Pod Ice Cream

12 egg yolks
250g caster sugar
1 vanilla pod
800ml whole milk
360ml double cream

Chocolate Sauce

150g good quality dark chocolate
1/2 pint double cream
50g caster sugar

Rhubarb And Apple Compôte

2 sticks of rhubarb
1 Bramley cooking apple
1 cinnamon stick
40g caster sugar
10g butter

Method

For The Bread And Butter Pudding

Line a baking tray with greaseproof paper. Separate four eggs and keep two whole. Mix with caster sugar. Slice and butter croissants and pain au chocolat then layer onto a tray with chocolate chips. Bring double cream to a boil with a vanilla pod and add to egg and sugar mix. Pour the mixture over the croissants and pain au chocolat and allow to soak for 20 minutes. Cover and place in oven at 180°C for 20 minutes.

For The Vanilla Pod Ice Cream

Separate egg yolks and mix with sugar. Heat milk, cream and vanilla in a pan. Let the vanilla pod infuse then pass through a sieve onto the egg mix. Whisk together and return to a gentle heat. Stir until the mix is coating the back of a wooden spoon. Pass again through a sieve and allow to cool before churning.

> **Chef's Tip**
> Use a heavy bottomed pan for ice cream as it will stop the mix sticking.

For The Chocolate Sauce

Warm through the double cream, then add the chocolate. Stir until melted then mix in the caster sugar.

For The Rhubarb And Apple Compôte

Peel the rhubarb and dice into 1cm cubes. Peel the apple, core and dice. Add 10g butter to a pan over a low heat, add apple, rhubarb and cinnamon stick and sweat until soft. Add caster sugar and cook on low heat for 20 minutes.

To Serve

Portion the pudding into equal squares. Serve with a scoop of ice cream, place the rhubarb and apple compôte on top of the drizzled chocolate sauce.

230
WEDGWOOD
THE RESTAURANT

Royal Mile, 267 Canongate, Edinburgh, EH8 8BQ

0131 558 8737
www.wedgwoodtherestaurant.co.uk twitter: @chefwedgwood

Wedgwood the restaurant is now firmly established as one of the country's top eateries. Combining fine dining in unpretentious surroundings, complemented by stellar service has helped this restaurant gain a reputation which it justly deserves - gathering rave reviews from industry professionals, tourists and informed locals, as well as scooping a raft of awards and accolades along the way. Situated on Edinburgh's Royal Mile, this stylish establishment is the brainchild of Paul Wedgwood and Lisa Channon who have created what would be their own perfect night out. Paul's style of food is arguably unique with plays on classics such as the signature lobster thermidor crème brûlée, or a deliciously different chicken Caesar salad soup.

Lisa's style of service is warm and friendly yet professional, slick and unobtrusive. Together this young couple have created one of Scotland's must dine destinations. Local produce is the focus of the ever changing menus with an inspirational use of foraged ingredients, many of which Paul forages for himself. Using local farms to source organic lamb, mutton and other menu items ensures guests truly get to taste some of the best the Scottish larder has to offer.

Awards and accolades have come thick and fast in the first five years of opening. In 2010, they were awarded 'Best New Restaurant in the UK' in the Harden's Restaurant Guide and voted 'Scottish Restaurant of the year' for two years running in 2010 and 2011 by SLTN.

Photography by Darren McKean

Celebrating
5 Years
of Wedgwood
the Restaurant

Wedgwood is listed by the Sunday Times as being one of the top ten places to dine in Scotland for the last two years, has received Fodors choice award for the last three years and is naturally listed in the Michelin guide.

WILD SEA TROUT, SCALLOP & BUNNAHABHAIN WHISKY TARTARE, ORANGE, VANILLA, CUCUMBER, DILL

SERVES 4

Little Beauty Pinot Gris, Marlborough NZ 2010
(New Zealand)

Method

Mix together orange juice, whisky and vanilla pod with a touch of salt and pepper.

Combine the diced cucumber, scallops and sea trout in a bowl.

Pour whisky over the mix and stir.

Add dill and pieces of orange segments.

Adjust seasoning and serve immediately in a glass.

Chef's Tip

As the fish for this dish is essentially raw it is imperative to get the freshest fish possible. Tell your fishmonger about the dish you are creating in advance and he can source you the freshest fish for the day you need it.

Ingredients

300g wild sea trout fillet (diced)
4 medium diver-caught king scallops (cleaned and diced)
$^1/_2$ cucumber (peeled and diced, reserve peel)

$^1/_2$ large orange (peeled, reserve 2 segments and squeeze juice from rest)
25ml Bunnahabhain 12 years old whisky
1 vanilla pod (scraped)
dill
salt and pepper

VENISON, ITS OWN HAGGIS SPIKED WITH BUNNAHABHAIN WHISKY, CREAMED LEEKS, PICKLED SQUASH, HERBED BARLEY, TRUFFLE JUS

SERVES 4

 Mencia Pittacum, Bierzo 2006
(Spain)

Ingredients

Venison

4 x 250g pieces venison loin

500g venison haggis (mixed with 50ml Bunnahabhain whisky)

Barley
100g barley
4 sprigs rosemary
6 sprigs thyme

Pickled Squash

200ml white wine vinegar
500ml water
100g sugar
$^{1}/_{2}$ cinnamon stick
2 star anise
400g butternut squash (cut into 1.5cm cubes)

Truffle Jus
5ml white truffle oil
200ml venison *jus*

Creamed Leeks
2 leeks (chopped)
200ml double cream
salt and pepper

2 floury potatoes (diced)
oil (for frying)

Method

Preheat oven to 200°C

For The Creamed Leeks
Gently fry the leeks until soft, add cream and reduce until thick, season to taste.

For The Venison
In a hot pan seal, off the venison and then place in oven for eight minutes. Cook for longer if you like it more than medium rare. Turn over the venison to ensure even cooking and return to the oven. When cooked to your preference, remove from oven, season, then leave somewhere warm and allow to rest for four minutes.

For The Potatoes
Deep fry the diced potatoes until golden and crisp.

For The Truffle Jus
Heat the *jus* and add the truffle oil, whisk well to incorporate.

For The Haggis
Heat haggis through in the oven until piping hot, then mould in a metal mousse ring about half full, top with the creamed leeks.

For The Pickled Squash (Prepare two days in advance)
In a heavy bottomed pan, bring to a boil the vinegar, sugar and water. Dry roast the cinnamon and star anise for about 15 seconds. Add these to the vinegar mixture along with the butternut squash and bring to a boil. Set aside to cool. Place in a kilner jar in the fridge for two days

For The Herbed Barley
Soak in cold water overnight, drain then place in a heavy bottomed pan and fill with water. Add the sprigs of rosemary and thyme and cook until tender.

To Serve
Arrange the herbed barley, pickled squash and crisp potatoes around the plate. Drizzle with truffle *jus*.

Remove the metal mould from the haggis and leeks. Slice the rested venison in half and place on either side of the haggis and leeks.

BUNNAHABHAIN WHISKY & HONEY ROAST PARSNIP CREME BRULEE, THYME ICE CREAM

SERVES 6

 *Late Harvest Gewurtraminer, Montes,
Curico Valley, 2010 (Chile)*

Ingredients

Crème Brûlée

2 medium sized parsnips (to make 500g purée)
6 large egg yolks and 1 whole egg
75g caster sugar (plus extra to glaze)
1 tsp vegetable oil
1 tbsp honey
600ml double cream
50ml Bunnahabhain 12 years old whisky
6 x 4oz ramekins

Thyme Ice Cream

8 egg yolks
175g caster sugar
500ml milk
500ml double cream
20g fresh thyme leaves
5g fried, fresh thyme leaves

Method

For The Parsnip Crème Brûlée

Peel and core parsnips and cut into 2cm dice. Place on a baking sheet with oil and honey, cover with foil and bake for about 20 minutes at 180°C until soft. Leave to cool.

Place cream and whisky into a thick bottom pan and bring to a boil. In the meantime, cream together eggs and sugar until light and fluffy.

Pour over a little of the hot cream mix to 'scald' the egg mix then add the rest of the cream.

In a food processor, blitz together the parsnips and brûlée mix and pass through a fine sieve. Keep working as much of the mix through as possible.

Skim off any foam. Pour into ramekins. Place into a *bain-marie* in a warm oven for about 10 to 15 minutes.

For The Thyme Ice Cream

Beat egg yolks and sugar until pale in colour.

Mix milk, cream and fresh thyme in a heavy bottomed pan and bring to a boil.

Simmer for five minutes, take off heat and cool for 30 seconds.

Pour milk mix onto egg mix whisking continuously.

Return to pan and cook on LOW heat until mixture coats the back of spoon.

Strain through a very fine sieve and leave to cool. Add fried thyme leaves.

Churn till nearly set.

To Serve

Glaze each of the parsnip custards with a dusting of caster sugar and, with the aid of a chefs blow torch, gently brûlée each custard being careful not to burn the sugar. Present alongside the thyme ice cream.

RELISH SCOTLAND LARDER

BAKERY

CAMPBELL'S BAKERY LTD.
59 King Street, Crieff, Perthshire, PH7 3HB
T: 01764 652114

Established in 1830, Campbell's Bakery is Scotland's oldest independent family run craft bakery. As well as traditional Scottish favourites such as scotch pies, oatcakes and shortbread, Campbell's Bakery also produces an inspired range of breads and cakes, including black olive ciabatta, carrot and linseed, granary cob, lemon and dill and pumpkin seed loaf.

Bunnahabhain Whisky

The Restaurant At The Lovat

BEVERAGES

BUNNAHABHAIN WHISKY
Burn Stewart Distillers Ltd
Bunnahabhain Distillery, Port Askaig,
Isle of Islay, PA46 7RP
www.bunnahabhain.com
Twitter: BunnahabhainWhisky - @Bunnahabhain

Bunnahabhain is the flagship malt Scotch whisky from Burn Stewart Distillers and is exported to over 30 countries globally.

TOBERMORY MALT WHISKY
Tobermory Distillery, Ledaig, Tobermory, Isle of Mull
T: 01688 302 645
www.tobermorymalt.com

Crafted, nurtured and aged by islanders since 1798, Tobermory is simply one of Mull's hidden gems. Each bottle has been rested on Mull awaiting its time and when bottled it becomes something which can only be described as treasure.

WOODWINTERS WINES AND WHISKIES LTD
16 Henderson Street, Bridge of Allan, Scotland, FK9 4HP
91 Newington Road, Edinburgh, EH9 1QW
T: 01786 834 894/0131 6672 760
Mon-Sat 10am-7pm, Sun 1pm-5pm

IWSC UK Independent Wine Merchant of the Year 2010 and IWC Scottish Wine Merchant of the Year 2006, 2207 and 2009.

COOK SCHOOLS

CLAIRE MACDONALD
Kinloch Lodge, Sleet, Isle of Skye, IV43 8QY
T: 01471 833 333
www.claire-macdonald.com

COOK SCHOOL BY MARTIN WISHART
14 Bonnington Road, Edinburgh, EH6 5JD.
0131 5556 655
www.martin-wishart.co.uk

NICK NAIRN COOK SCHOOL
Port of Monteith, Stirling, FK8 3JZ
01877 389 900
www.nicknairncookschool.com

COOKWARE AND TABLEWARE

HIGHLAND STONEWARE
Lochinver, Sutherland, IV27 4LP
T: 01571 844 376
www.highlandstoneware.com

Handmade and individually painted pottery from the Highlands of Scotland.

For more food producers and suppliers in Scotland please visit **www.tasteofscotland.com**

DAIRY

CLARKS SPECIALITY FOODS
Artisan Cheeses
202 Bruntsfield Place, Edinburgh, EH10 4DF
T: 0844 3356 908
www.clarksfoods.co.uk

Clarks is a gourmet's delight focussing on farmhouse and artisan cheese, supplying over 300 types of cheese from around the UK and Europe. Suppliers of many other quality products.

GRAHAM'S THE FAMILY DAIRY
Airthrey Kerse Farm, Henderson Street,
Bridge of Allan, FK9 4RW
T: 01786 833 206
www.grahamsfamilydairy.com

Scottish dairy products including milk, butter and cream from Graham's Scottish Dairies.

Katy Rodger

KATY RODGER'S ARTISAN DAIRY
Knockraich Farm, Fintry, Stirlingshire, G63 0LN
T: 01360 860 202
www.knockraich.com

A small family run dairy producing Scotland's finest natural yoghurts, crème fraiche, crowdie, ice creams and frozen yoghurt.

Winner of the Scotland Food and Drink 'Product of the Year 2012'

FINE AND SPECIALITY FOODS

LETTERFINLAY FINE FOODS
Units 1 & 2 Annat Industrial Estate, Corpach,
Fort William, PH33 7NA
T: 01397 772957

For meats and speciality goods.

MACKINTOSH OF GLENDAVENY
Glendaveny, Peterhead, Aberdeenshire, AB42 3E
T: 07876 474 546
www.mackintoshofglendaveny.co.uk

*Extra virgin, cold pressed rapeseed oil, home grown, pressed
and bottled in Aberdeenshire. 100% free from chemicals
and preservatives.*

The Peat Inn

21212

MARK MURPHY AND PARTNER LTD
Unit 2 Newbridge Industrial Estate, Newbridge
Midlothian, EH28 8PJ
T: 0131 3353 040
www.markmurphyltd.co.uk

*Suppliers of premium quality fruit and vegetables, dairy
products as well as exotics and fine foods.*

STRATHSPEY MUSHROOMS
Unit 4 A3, Strathspey Industrial Estate, Woodlads Terrace,
Grantown on Spey, PH26 3NB
T: 01479 873 344
www.getdeli.co.uk

Wonderful Scottish mushrooms and deli products.

FISH

AJ DUNCAN (DIVING SERVICES)
Leven
T: 07867 794 040

Supplier of hand-dived scallops.

ALFIE EDWARDS
Burnside, Camusterrach, Applecross, IV54 8LT
T: 01520 744 313

*Alfie is a local fish supplier who can supply most fish,
shellfish and local fruit and vegetables, all when in season.
Van deliveries in a regulated chiller van.*

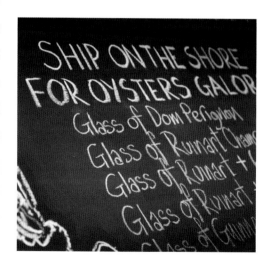

Squat Lobster, Loch Ness Inn

DAVID LOWRIE
Fish Merchant
St Monan's
T: 01333 730 770

Supplier of fish and shellfish.

GEORGE CAMPBELL AND SON
Perth
T: 01738 638 454

Supplier of fish and shellfish.

GOURLINE FISH MERCHANTS
West Quay, Gourdon, Montrose, Angus, DD10 0NA
T: 01561 361 545
www.gourline.co.uk

Fresh haddock, sole, plaice and cod caught by their own vessels and landed on their doorstep at West Quay allows them to ensure their fish are the freshest available.

In addition to their merchant service, they are pleased to offer a smoking facility - through a traditional kiln process. They smoke any form of seafood overnight.

HAND-DIVED HIGHLAND SHELLFISH
(Andrew Reid)
T: 07899 995 600
www.highlandshellfish.co.uk

Provide the best live scallops from the west coast. Dived for and delivered within 24 hours.

ISLE OF MULL CRAB COMPANY
Croig, Dervaig, Isle of Mull
T: 01688 400 364
www.mullcrab.co.uk

A small family-run business specialising in fresh hand-picked crab meat. The secret of Isle of Mull crab is the fresh quality of the crab as it is caught daily aboard the creel boat 'Eilean Ban'. Once caught, the best of the catch is selected to be hand-picked for the local market.

LOCH DUART SALMON
Badcall Salmon House, Scourie, Lairg,
Sutherland, IV27 4TH
T: 01670 660 161
www.lochduart.com

The difference begins with their approach to rearing salmon and ends with a product which is consistently judged superior in taste, quality, colour and overall perception, as evidenced by the number of international leading chefs and restaurants which service Loch Duart farmed salmon by name.

STEVE COOPER AT SRC FOODS
15 Ladysmith Street, Ullapool,
Ross-shire, IV26 2UW
T: 01854 613 020
www.srcfoods.com

Independent seafood supplier and wholesaler based in Ullapool on the west coast of The Highlands of Scotland - home to some of the finest shellfish and seafood in the world.

TOBERMORY FISH FARM
Baliscate, Tobermory, Isle of Mull
T: 01688 302 120

TOSCAIG SHELLFISH (ALI MACLEOD)
The Schoolhouse, Applecross, IV54 8LT
T: 01520 744348
fishermanapx@btinternet.com

*Creel-caught Applecross Bay prawns and squat lobsters
orders taken subject to weather conditions.*

WILLIE-FISH
8 Stevenson Street, Oban, Argyll, Scotland, PA34 5NA
T: 01631 567 156
www.williefishoban.co.uk

*A wide range of seafood and shellfish, including scallops,
razor clams, oysters, smoked salmon and trout, as well as
smoked fish pate. As far as possible, all their fish is sourced
locally but they are happy to track down any variety not
readily available.*

Nick Nairn Cook School

MEAT AND POULTRY

THE ABERFOYLE BUTCHER
206 Main Street, Aberfoyle, FK8 3UQ
T: 01877 382 473
www.aberfoylebutcher.co.uk

*An independent butcher cradled in the heart of the
Trossachs. They can supply directly to your kitchen, whether
it's an exquisite restaurant, hotel or if you simply appreciate
the finest food at home.*

APPLECROSS ESTATE LARDER
Applecross House, Applecross, IV54 8ND
T: 01520 744 247
www.applecrossestatetrust.org

*Prime venison carcass, shot on the peninsula and hung in
the larder until in prime condition.*

The Ship On The Shore Seafood Restaurant & Champagne Bar

Applecross Inn

The Byzantium

BEL'S BUTCHER
25a High Street, Edzell, Angus, DD9 7TE
T: 01356 648 409

Excellent Angus beef and black pudding to meet your specific requirements.

BRAEHEAD FOODS
7 Moorfields North Industrial Park, Crosshouse,
Kilmarnock KA2 0FE
T: 0156 550 008
www.braeheadfoods.co.uk

Leading purveyor of speciality foods and game.

CAMPBELL'S PRIME MEAT
The Heatherfield, Haining Road,
Lathallen (by Linlithgow), EH49 6LQ
T: 01506 858 585
www.campbellsmeat.com

Suppliers of 28 day matured beef, fish and shellfish.

D&A KENNEDY
36 High Street, Blairgowrie - T: 01250 870 358
12 Castle Street, Forfar - T: 01307 462 118
www.kennedybeef.com

Finest locally sourced livestock from Forfar market.

GREAT GLEN GAME
The Old Butcher's Shop, Roy Bridge, PH33 4AE
T: 01397 712 121
www.greatglengame.co.uk

For wild venison and preserved meats.

JOHN HENDERSON MEAT
Unit 8, Fife, Glenrothes, KY6 2RU
T: 01592 770 555
jhenderson@ic24.net

David and Andrew offer quality and customer care and are always keen to offer fresh ideas.

MACDONALD BROTHER'S BUTCHERS
Pitlochry
T: 01796 472 047
www.macdonald-bros.co.uk

Family business run by Rory Macdonald supplying top quality meat, poultry and game.

Loch Ness Inn

MACBETH'S BUTCHERS

11 Tolbooth Street, Forres, IV36 1PH
T: 01309 672 254
www.macbeths.com

Traditional Scottish butcher and game dealer.

MACPHAIL'S ISLE OF MULL VENISON

Woodside Croft, Salen, Isle of Mull
T: 01680 300 220

PEELHAM FARM

Foulden, Berwickshire, TD15 1UG
T: 01890 781 328
www.peelham.co.uk

*Peelham Farm have ethical producing values and
superior quality beef, lamb and pork. Chris and Denise
Walton run an amazing farm, rearing the animals from
birth to butcher so that they are in complete control of
the product from start to finish.*

SIMON HOWIE

The Scottish Butcher
Simon Howie Foods, Findony, Muckhart Road Dunning,
Perthshire, PH2 0RA
T: 01764 684 332
enquiries@simonhowiefoods.co.uk
www.simonhowiefoods.co.uk

*Supplier of haggis, fine quality meats and ready meals to
public and restaurants*

WE HAE MEAT

66a Dalrymple Street, Girvan, Ayrshire, KA26 9BT
T: 01465 713 366
www.wehaemeat.com

*Family run butcher's business owned by Girvan
farmer Alex Paton. Alex's farming experience allows him
to select animals that are reared in the best way to
maximise the taste and quality of the meat.*

SMOKED FOODS

FEOCHAN MHOR SMOKEHOUSE

Kilmore, Oban, Argyll, PA34 4XT
T: 01631 770 670
www.feochanmhorsmokehouse.co.uk

*Delicious smoked fish, patés and shellfish from the
smokehouse. Also fresh fish and shellfish from their shop
in Oban.*

GALLOWAY SMOKEHOUSE

Carsluith, Newton Stewart, DG8 7DN
T: 01671 820 354
www.gallowaysmokehouse.co.uk

*All foods are cured with salt before smoking and,
to give a fuller flavour, they add dark syrup and black
rum to the salmon. Their prize-winning smoked foods
are a gourmet's delight.*

The Dining Room

VEGETABLES AND FRUIT

MARK MURPHY & PARTNER LTD

Unit 2 Newbridge Industrial Estate,
Newbridge, Midlothian, EH28 8PJ
T: 0131 335 3040
www.markmurphyltd.co.uk
Facebook: /markmurpyltd.co.uk
Twitter: /markmurphyltd
enquiries@markmurphyltd.co.uk

*Established in 1981 and now employs over 90 staff.
Open all day, every day. Their large fleet of refrigerated
vehicles deliver across Edinburgh, the central belt, the
borders and part of the highlands.*

*Suppliers of premium quality fruit and vegetables, dairy
products and fine foods, with a great deal of experience
as well as a comprehensive understanding of the
catering trade's requirements. Because they understand
the catering trade, deliveries are made six days a week,
with a back up supply on Sundays to Edinburgh City.*

The Peat Inn

MACLEOD ORGANICS

Kylerona Farm, 8 Hillhead, Ardersier, IV2 7QZ
T:. 01667 462 555
www.macleodorganics.co.uk

*A family firm that has been delivering since October
1998 with a proud history. Fully committed to bringing
the freshest, local and 100% organic products to
your doorstep.*

WILLIAMSON GROUP LTD

5 Walker Road, Longman Industrial Estate,
Inverness, IV1 1TD
T: 01463 236 600

*Suppliers of fresh fruit, salad, vegetables, dairy, deli
and dry goods. Will always help to source requirements.
Good on local food.*

The Seafood Restaurant

Killiecrankie Hotel

Paul Kitching, 21212

Craig Millar, Craig Millar @ 16 West End

21212
3 Royal Terrace
Edinburgh, EH7 5AB
0845 22 21212
www.21212restaurant.co.uk

THE AIRDS HOTEL & RESTAURANT
Port Appin, Appin
Argyll, PA38 4DF
01631 730 095
www.airds-hotel.com

APPLECROSS INN
Shore Street, Applecross
Strathcarron, Wester Ross, IV54 8LR
01520 744 262
www.applecross.uk.com

BALLATHIE COUNTRY HOUSE HOTEL & ESTATE
Kinclaven, Stanley
Perthshire, PH1 4QN
01250 883 268
www.ballathiehousehotel.com

THE BYZANTIUM
11 Hawkhill
Dundee, DD1 5DL
01382 221946
www.byzantiumrestaurant.com

CRAIG MILLAR @ 16 WEST END
16 West End, St Monans
Fife, KY10 2BX
01333 730 327
www.16westend.com

Mattia Camorani, Cucina

Mark Easton, Killiecrankie Hotel

CRINGLETIE HOUSE
Edinburgh Road
Peebles, EH45 8PL
01721 725 750
www.cringletie.com

CUCINA
Hotel Missoni, 1 George IV Bridge
Edinburgh, EH1 1AD
0131 220 6666
www.hotelmissoni.com

THE DINING ROOM
28 Queen Street
Edinburgh, EH2 1JX
0131 220 2044
www.thediningroomedinburgh.co.uk   www.smws.co.uk

HAMILTON'S BAR & KITCHEN
16–18 Hamilton Place
Stockbridge, Edinburgh, EH3 5AU
0131 226 4199
www.hamiltonsedinburgh.co.uk

KILLIECRANKIE HOTEL
Killiecrankie, By Pitlochry
Perthshire, PH16 5LG
01796 473 220
www.killiecrankiehotel.co.uk

THE KITCHIN
78 Commercial Street
Edinburgh, Midlothian, EH6 6LX
0131 555 1755
www.thekitchin.com

250
CONTRIBUTORS

Paul Gunning, Purslane

Geoffrey Smeddle, The Peat Inn

LIME TREE AN EALDHAIN
Achintore Road
Fort William, PH33 6RQ
01397 701 806
www.limetreefortwilliam.co.uk

LOCH NESS INN
Lewiston, Drumnadrochit
Inverness-shire, IV63 6UW
01456 450 991
www.staylochness.co.uk

NICK NAIRN COOK SCHOOL
Port of Menteith
Stirling, FK8 3JZ
01877 389 900
www.nairnscookschool.com

THE PEAT INN
Cupar
Fife, KY15 5LH
01334 840 206
www.thepeatinn.co.uk

PURSLANE
33a St Stephen Street, Stockbridge
Edinburgh, EH3 5AH
0131 226 3500
www.purslanerestaurant.co.uk

THE RESTAURANT AT THE LOVAT
Loch Ness, Fort Augustus
Inverness-shire, PH32 4DU
01456 459 250
www.thelovat.com

Mark Greenaway, Restaurant Mark Greenaway

Paul Wedgwood, Wedgwood The Restaurant

RESTAURANT MARK GREENAWAY
69 North Castle Street
Edinburgh EH2 3LJ
0131 226 115
www.restaurantmarkgreenaway.com

ROCCA BAR & GRILL
The Links, St Andrews
Fife, KY16 9JQ
01334 472 549
www.roccagrill.com

THE SEAFOOD RESTAURANT
Bruce Embankment, St Andrews
Fife, KY16 9AB
01334 479 475
www.theseafoodrestaurant.com

THE SHIP ON THE SHORE
SEAFOOD RESTAURANT & CHAMPAGNE BAR
24-26 Shore
Edinburgh, EH6 6QN
0131 555 0409
www.theshiponthshore.co.uk

WEDGWOOD THE RESTAURANT
Royal Mile,
267 Canongate
Edinburgh, EH8 8BQ
0131 558 8737
www.wedgwoodtherestaurant.co.uk

RELISH PUBLICATIONS

Relish Publications is an independent publisher of exclusive regional cook books, featuring only the best and brightest critically acclaimed chefs and the venues at which they work, all of which showcased with superb photography. They also work with some chefs individually to produce bespoke publications tailored to their individual specifications. Since 2009, Relish has fostered a national presence, while maintaining friendly, personalised service that their small but highly professional team prides themselves on.

Visit www.relishpublications.co.uk and check out the series of high quality cook books.

Relish Midlands

As the geographical heart of the country and one of its most densely populated areas, the Midlands has so much to offer in terms of amazing food that blends a variety of styles and influences. The Michelin starred Andreas Antona introduces us to 26 of the best restaurants in the UK.

Relish Wales

A region with its own rich, unique heritage and home to a vast and diverse landscape. From the rugged valleys and endless coastlines to the bustling streets of Cardiff and it's other big cities, Welsh cuisine represents a blend of cultures that is as interesting as it is delicious. Renowned chef Shaun Hill introduces this ambitious book that covers the wide range of talent that Wales has to offer.

Relish Greater Manchester and Cheshire

As one of the most populated areas in the UK, Greater Manchester has a wealth of talent to display. Traditionally seen as a historic centre of industry, Manchester's finer side inspires great chefs such as Andrew Nutter to produce truly amazing food. Alongside this, Cheshire offers a refreshing change of pace. Further away from the hustle and bustle, its own character is reflected in some equally stunning cuisine. This Relish book shows it all in this journey around the North West.

Relish Merseyside and Lancashire

As one of the most historically significant ports in the country, Liverpool continues to have importance to this day, by giving us all access to a world of high quality food, but there is just as much talent further afield, as shown in the stunning chefs we have chosen to represent Lancashire. Renowned local chef, Paul Askew, starts off this book by introducing us to some of the quality produce that this region has to offer, and how he is so proud to be championing an area that has many great chefs and restaurants.

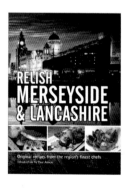

252

RELISH SCOTLAND SECOND HELPING

Relish Yorkshire Second Helping

The latest edition of Relish Yorkshire features a foreword by celebrity chef Tessa Bramley and returns to the county with all new recipes from Yorkshire's greatest chefs; Michelin starred James McKenzie from The Pipe and Glass and Steve Smith from The Burlington, plus Richard Allen from The Fourth Floor at Harvey Nichols and many, many more. Relish Yorkshire Second Helping is a must have for any hearty food lover with true Yorkshire pride.

Relish Scotland Volume 1

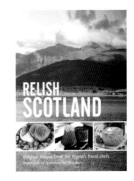

With over 300 pages of Scotland's finest recipes, this book takes you on an epic journey from Edinburgh to Glasgow, across to Aberdeen and then up to the Highlands and Islands, through rugged landscapes and beautiful cities. An introduction from TV celebrity chef Nick Nairn prepares the palate for recipes from nationally acclaimed restaurateurs such as Tom Kitchin, Martin Wishart and Geoffrey Smeddle. With breathtaking pictures of the views and venues, Relish Scotland promises to make for fascinating reading for both foodies and tourists alike.

Relish Cumbria Volume 1

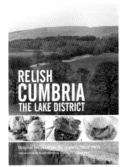

Over 50 mouth-watering exclusive recipes for you to try at home from some of Cumbria's finest Country House Hotels and acclaimed restaurants including Nigel Mendham at The Samling, Russell Plowman at Gilpin Lodge Hotel and Andrew McGeorge at Rampsbeck Country House Hotel. Packed with innovative recipes and stunning photography to match the stunning landscape, Relish Cumbria is certain to make a fantastic addition to any cook's library.

Relish Cumbria Second Helping

This second exciting edition features a foreword by Michelin-starred David McLaughlin with all new exclusive recipes from a selection of Cumbria's finest country house hotels and acclaimed restaurants. New entries include Holbeck Ghyll, The Punch Bowl Inn and The Wordsworth Hotel with old favourites such as The Samling and Merewood Country House Hotel making a welcome return. With stunning photography, innovative recipes and a host of exclusive chefs tips, this latest edition takes you on a foodie journey that will delight your taste buds and test your culinary skills in equal measure.

Relish North East

From the bustling city life in Newcastle, to the multitude of sleepy, rural villages, the North East has something for everyone. An introduction from the North East's best known chef, Terry Laybourne, kicks off this culinary adventure through a rich and diverse region, with many varied recipes for you to try at home including a selection from the North East's two Masterchef finalists, John Calton and David Coulson, plus many others from award-winning chefs across the region.

Relish
PUBLICATIONS

LOOKING TO DINE IN THE UK'S FINEST RESTAURANTS?

Visit the Relish Restaurant Guide to find the very best your region has to offer.

The Relish team has worked with all of the restaurants and chefs listed on the Relish website and have visited every highly recommended and acclaimed restaurant. These ingredients make the **Relish Restaurant Guide** genuine and unique.

If you would like to be taken on an epic journey to the finest restaurants in each region, to download more mouth-watering recipes, to join our exclusive Relish Rewards club, or to add to your collection of Relish books, visit **www.relishpublications.co.uk**

WHAT'S APP-ENING?

Our series of regional cook books are now available to download and purchase.

Browse 100s of recipes with beautiful photography and easy to follow instructions from a selection of the UK's finest chefs and restaurants.

 Download now on the App Store/Relish Cookbook.

Apple, the Apple logo and iPhone are trademarks of Apple Inc, registered in the US and other countries, App Store is a service mark of Apple Inc.

GLOSSARY

BAIN-MARIE
A pan or other container of hot water with a bowl placed on top of it. This allows the steam from the water to heat the bowl so ingredients can be gently heated or melted in the bowl.

BEURRE BLANC
French translates as 'white butter'. A hot emulsified butter sauce made with a reduction of vinegar and/or white wine (normally Muscadet) and grey shallots. Cold, whole butter is blended off the heat to prevent separation.

BLANCH
Boiling an ingredient before removing it and plunging it in ice cold water in order to stop the cooking process.

BRUNOISE
A culinary knife cut in which the food item is first julienned and then turned a quarter turn and diced again, producing cubes of about 3mm or less on each side.

CHINOIS
A conical sieve with an extremely fine mesh. It is used to strain custards, purées, soups and sauces, producing a very smooth texture.

CLARIFIED BUTTER
Milk fat rendered from butter to separate the milk solids and water from the butter fat.

COMPOTE
French for 'mixture'. Whole fruits are cooked in water with sugar and spices. The syrup may be seasoned and can be served either warm or cold.

CONFIT
A method of cooking where the meat is cooked and submerged in a liquid to add flavour. Often this liquid is rendered fat.

CREPINETTE
Crépine is the French word for 'pig's caul' in which a crépinette is wrapped instead of a casing.

DARIOLE
A French term that refers to small, cylinder shaped moulds.

DEGLAZE
A fancy term for using the flavour-packed brown bits stuck to the bottom of a pan to make a pan sauce or gravy.

DEHYDRATE
Drying is a method of food preservation that works by removing water from the food. Food dehydrators are available in most cook shops.

EMULSION/EMULSIFY
In the culinary arts, an emulsion is a mixture of two liquids that would ordinarily not mix together, like oil and vinegar.

JUS
The natural juices given off by the food. To prepare a natural jus, the cook may simply skim off the fat from the juices left after cooking and bring the remaining meat stock and water to a boil.

LIQUOR
The liquid that is left over from the cooking of meat or vegetables. Can be incorporated into sauces and gravy.

MIREPOIX
Combination of celery (pascal, celery or celeriac), onions, and carrots. There are many regional mirepoix variations, which can sometimes be just one of these ingredients, or include additional spices. See The Dining Room's version on page 94.

MONTE
Sauce finishing. Adding small quantities of butter (emulsify) to thicken a sauce.

PANE
To coat with flour, beaten egg and breadcrumbs.

REDUCTION
The process of thickening a liquid in order to intensify the flavour. This is done by evaporating the moisture in a liquid.

SABAYON
A sabayon is made by beating egg yolks with a liquid over simmering water until thickened and increased in volume. The liquid can be water, but Champagne or wine is often used for a savoury sabayon.

SHUCKED (OYSTERS)
Shucked oysters are those that have been removed from their shells. To learn how to shuck an oyster you can always visit Nick Nairn's Cook School!

SEEDING/TEMPERED (CHOCOLATE)
'Tempering is like organising individual dancers at a party into a Conga line. For chocolate, temperature and motion are the party organisers that bring all the individual dancing crystals of fatty acids together in long lines and, in the process, create a stable crystallisation throughout the chocolate mass'. Chocomap.com

Dessert, Purslane